SHE LOST HER FIRST FAMILY AND BECAME A SINGLE MOTHER LONG BEFORE SHE BECAME "DR. RUTH"

Dr. Ruth Westheimer shows why family values are much more difficult to define than the politicians want you to believe, how you can make your family more nurturing and supportive, and how our society must change to ensure the future health of children, parents, and all those who are willing to nurture, love, and care.

"What gives this volume impact is the breadth of Dr. Ruth's personal experience and the succinct and sensible marshaling of material....Dr. Ruth's advice on sex has helped create new ideas about relationships; this feisty work may help stiffen the spines of the inventive men and women who are now trying to redefine the American family."

—*Kirkus Reviews*

"Dr. Ruth Westheimer has written a very real and honest account of family values as they are today. This is an easy-reading, direct, and informative, oftentimes anecdotal view of where the family is now. Another wonderful direction for Dr. Ruth to be moving toward."

—Ira M. Sacker, M.D., director, Adolescent Medicine and Eating Disorders, Brookdale University Hospital Medical Center, and author of *Dying to Be Thin*

"There is much wisdom here....It provides humane, well-reasoned, and often well-supported arguments and delivers them in an informal style. They counter moralistic sound bites about social decay and loss of traditional values with a view of the American family that is broad, complex, and affirming."

—*Philadelphia Inquirer*

THE VALUE of VALUE

THE VALUE of FAMILY

A BLUEPRINT FOR THE 21st CENTURY

DR. RUTH WESTHEIMER
AND BEN YAGODA

WARNER BOOKS

A Time Warner Company

Grateful acknowledgment is made to the following for permission to reprint from copyrighted materials: "Public and Private: Playing Perfect Pattycake," by Anna Quindlen. Copyright © 1994 by the New York Times Company. Reprinted by permission. *Parents Express* interview with Penelope Leach reprinted by permission of *Parents Express* and the *Philadelphia Inquirer*. "Made in Heaven: Meet the DiNapolis," by Murray Dubin, reprinted by permission of the *Philadelphia Inquirer*.

Warner Books, Inc. 1271 Avenue of the Americas, New York, N.Y. 10020
Visit our Web site at
http://pathfinder.com/twep

Printed in the United States of America
First Trade Printing: August 1997
10 9 8 7 6 5 4 3 2 1

Library of Congress Cataloging-in-Publication Data
Westheimer, Ruth K.
    The value of family : a blueprint for the 21st century / Ruth Westheimer and Ben Yagoda.
        p.   cm.
    ISBN 0-446-67336-6
    1. Family—United States. 2. Social values—United States.
I. Yagoda, Ben.   II Title.
HQ536.W445   1996
306.85'0973—dc20
                                                                96-15154
                                                                    CIP

Book design by Giorgetta Bell McRee

To the memory of my entire family who perished during the Holocaust, thankful that they had the opportunity to instill in me the much cherished values of the Jewish tradition before they were lost to me. Also to my family of now: my husband Fred; daughter Miriam Westheimer, Ed.D., her husband Joel Einleger, and my grandson Ari; my son Joel Westheimer, Ph.D.; and two new additions to the family, daughter-in-law Barbara Leckie, Ph.D., and my granddaughter Leora Einleger. Hurray!
—R.W.

To my family—departed, present, and still to come.
—B.Y.

Acknowledgments

Pierre Lehu and I are now entering our fifteenth year of working together, and he is the best "Minister of Communications" that anybody could wish for. So a special toast to Pierre and to many more years of cooperation.

I want to thank the following people for adding so much to my life: Ruth Bachrach, Susan Brown and Frank Ciarkowski, Marian Wright Edelman, Martin Englisher, Howard and Dr. Cynthia Epstein, Yosh and Hannah Gafni, Rachel E. Gilon, Ellen Goldberg, David A. Goslin, Ph.D., Dennis and Brooks Holt, Fred Howard, Alfred Kaplan, Steven Kaplan, Ph.D., Michael and Ronnie Kassan, Bonnie Kaye, Richard and Barbara Kendall, Rabbi and Mrs. Leonard Kravitz, Marga and Bill Kunreuther, Marsha Lebby, Rabbi and Mrs. William Lebeau, Rabbi and Mrs. Robert Lehman, Joanne Lehu, Esq., Lou Lieberman, Ph.D., and Mary Cuadrado, John and Ginger Lollos, Jonathan and Ruchy Mark, Dale Ordes, Henry and Sydelle Ostberg, Robert Pinto, Fred and Ann Rosenberg, Cliff Rubin, Simeon and Rose Schreiber, Romie and Blanche Shapiro, Amir Shaviv, John and Marianne Slade, Rudi Steinbach, Robert Stewart, Hannah Strauss, and Greg Willenborg.

And a special thanks to the professionals at Warner Books

who helped make this book possible: Larry Kirshbaum, Susan Suffes, Letty Ferrando, Maureen Egen, Bob Castillo, Harvey-Jane Kowal, Karen Thompson, Thomas Whatley, Emi Battaglia, and Debbie Stier.

—R.W.

A heartfelt thank you to all the people who shared their expertise, their wisdom, and their lives, and in so doing made this book possible: Elijah Anderson, Mary Jo Bane, David Bianculli, David Blankenhorn, Maureen Byrnes, Stephanie Coontz, Wayne Cotter (for figuring out how a child could have five parents), Murray Dubin, Amitai Etzioni, Tom Ferrick, Frank Furstenberg, Lindy Giamattei, Vice President Al Gore, Katherine Hatton, Brian Hickey, Anndee Hochman, Len Jordan, Jeff Onore, Kathy Palomara, David Popenoe, Carol Rasko, Secretary of Education Richard Riley, Pepper Schwartz, Judith Stacey, Chuck Smith, Suzanna Smith, Susan E. Spock, Shari Thurer, Ione Vargus, Robin Warshaw, Miriam Westheimer, Henry Wiencek, Beatrice Wood, and Shirley Zimmerman.

And a special thanks to Dr. Ruth Westheimer, who through four projects has been thoughtful, intelligent, generous, and enthusiastic—the ideal collaborator.

—B.Y.

Contents

"I have found the one in whom my soul delights."

Song of Songs 3:4

Introduction

I decided to write a book about the American family because I felt it was an important topic. It was only after I began to do research, to read what the authorities had written and to listen to what a wide variety of people had to say that I realized that "important" didn't begin to describe it: In America today, family is gargantuan, all encompassing, inescapable.

The subject is on everybody's minds. Speaker of the House Newt Gingrich, picking up on a theme introduced by former Vice President Dan Quayle, goes on and on about "traditional family values" and their replacement by high divorce rates, two-career marriages, single mothers, and absent fathers—as if it were possible to will these trends away merely by denouncing them. (In view of his allegiance to the traditional nuclear family, Mr. Gingrich's advocacy of orphanages is a little puzzling. But more on that later.)

Ordinary Americans, meanwhile, are just as fixated. A recent national survey found that the overwhelming majority of Americans (90 percent of men and 92 percent of women) agree that the family is the most important institution in society. And, through a not necessarily sound logical process, we conclude that whenever anything is *wrong* in society, the family is at the root of the trouble. A 1994 *Wall Street Journal* poll revealed that the one thing blacks and whites agree on is that, next to crime, the number-one problem facing Americans is family breakdown. They do, however, disagree about the source of the breakdown: 53 percent of blacks blame financial pressures affecting families and 58 percent of whites blame "moral decline."

Debates about family have also been ringing out through our courtrooms. Every week, it seems, a new case makes the headlines where the central question is, What is a family? If a birth mother or father gives a child up for adoption and then at some later point reconsiders—as in the highly publicized cases of Baby Jessica and Baby Emily—do their rights outweigh those of the adoptive family with whom the child has been living? It would take a Solomon to decide—and unfortunately Solomons are in short supply nowadays.

New biomedical technology, whereby the participants in making a baby number far more than the traditional mom and dad, make these questions even more pressing and vexing. With artificial insemination, in vitro fertilization, and surrogate parents, one child can now have *five* parents at birth: the two who gave the cells, the mother who carried the child, and the two who raise it.

So debates about family are ubiquitous in taverns and coffee shops, congressional corridors and judicial chambers. But they also dominate our airwaves. Turn on the television and the odds are you'll see some kind of family, whether the Ozzie-and-Harriet-revisited world of *Home Improvement* or the less traditional versions seen in *Roseanne, Grace under Fire, Full House, Married . . . with Children, Family Matters, The Simpsons,* and, yes, *Murphy Brown.* You could even say that the workplace ensembles of *E.R.* and *N.Y.P.D. Blue* or the circle of friends featured in *Seinfeld* and *Ellen* are nothing other than disguised family units, sometimes functional, sometimes not.

And talk about dysfunctional! Daytime talk shows have turned into bizarre family-therapy sessions, with troubled clans airing their codependence and double binds for the whole country to see. Maybe the real secret to the success of Oprah and her kin is that they let the rest of us think that *our* family problems aren't so bad after all.

What about movies? Well, the top-grossing film of 1994—and one of the most successful films of all time—was *The Lion King*, which I saw with my then four-year-old grandson, Ari. One reason for its success, of course, was that it was a true family movie—a kids' film that parents could enjoy as well. But as Ari and I sat in the dark theater, hand in hand (except during the scary parts, when he put my hand over his eyes), it struck me that the film was also a parable *about* family and the disruption it is going through in the 1990s. After his uncle kills his father, the cub Simba goes off to live in the wilderness, where he is raised to manhood by a meerkat and a warthog. He only goes back to his mother when the ghost of his father says, "You must take your place in the circle of life." *There's* a nontraditional family for you!

Then there are films like *Mrs. Doubtfire* and *Junior*, hits that suggest that everything ailing the American family could be fixed if only the mothers could be cast aside and men could provide *all* the functions, be it housekeeper, caregiver, or fetus carrier.

Indeed, as long as you look beneath the surface (or listen to what the filmmakers have to say), you'll find that just about every recent movie is, deep down, about family. Consider these quotes:

"The movie is about family."—director Spike Lee, on *Crooklyn*

"This movie is about family, love and friendship."—director John Singleton, on *The Boyz N the Hood*

"It's a movie about family."—critic Hal Hinson, on *Terminator 2*

"This is a movie about family."—producer Michael Levy, on *Gardens of Stone*

Needless to say, the advertising industry is well aware of this family fixation. Whether it's pickup trucks, soup, orange juice, computers, housing developments, or long-distance phone service, nothing sells better than a glowing, idealized, often blond vision of the good old-fashioned nuclear American family.

We are so anxious about the family and children that, over and above the very real danger our kids face today, we make up still other, more gruesome perils. Studies have shown that the public perception of a growing threat of molestation and abduction of children bears little relation to reality, while the fear of Satanic sexual abuse is a complete invention.

So we talk, think, write, and more or less obsess about the family. Indeed, it sometimes seems as though we think of family not as real mothers and fathers and children, but as a kind of vessel or receptacle for all our societal concerns. We take all our hopes and dreams and anxieties, project them onto this almost mythical entity we call "the family," and all too often ignore the reality that is under our noses.

"We've always put a big burden on the family," says historian Stephanie Coontz, author of *The Way We Never Were: American Families and the Nostalgia Trap* and *The Social Origins of Private Life: A History of American Families 1600–1900.* "We expect more satisfactions and more accomplishments from the family than people in other societies do—we want it to be responsible for economic success, personal accomplishment, intelligence, moral values and our sense of contentment or happiness. Our society sets up high expectations that can't possibly be met—and so a large part of our popular culture attempts to meet them. There's a close relationship between the fact that America has the highest divorce rate in the world and the highest production of romance novels in the world. If, on the other hand, you live in a society that says that friendship, neighborhood groups, community, even extended family are all important—then a little bit of unhappiness in marriage is acceptable and you don't need to get your emotional sustenance from a paperback book.

"When there are bad outcomes with children, we blame it on the family, whether it's the genes or the environment they've provided. In most European societies, people are prepared to say, 'There are social classes, luck, structural things, all of which have a lot to do with the way a person turns out.' Here, it's the family."

Unfortunately, what Mark Twain said about another much-discussed topic, the weather, applies to the family as well: We don't really *do* much about it. For all the talk, all the debates, and all the hand-wringing, America treats its families and its children worse than almost any other developed country. The real threat to children isn't Satanic abduction but poverty. Our children are among the least likely in the world to be immunized, and the proportion of children living below the poverty line rose 49 percent from 1973 to 1992, to the point that in that year, no fewer than 25 percent of America's children were considered poor. (That figure would be even higher if the standard for poverty were more realistic than the current $15,355 annual income for a family of four.) In the years between 1973 and 1992, years of prosperity, the poorest 10 percent of American families suffered an 11 percent drop in real income.

Middle-class families don't confront those problems, but they do face the pressures of coping with a business culture and a government that, judging by their actions and policies, are indifferent if not actively hostile to families and children. These pressures have become especially striking in view of the huge demographic shift over the last few decades: the entry of women, including mothers, into the workplace on a massive and unprecedented scale. Currently, in about 70 percent of two-parent families, both spouses work at least part time, and in more than half of those cases, both spouses work full time. An even higher percentage of single mothers and fathers work (a surprising fact given all the publicity about welfare mothers living off the public dole). These families strongly need societal and institutional support, but they have not gotten much of it. No less than five years ago, just 3 percent of U.S. companies offered paid maternity leave and only 37 percent offered unpaid leave. In 1993, President Clinton had to fight to pass the Family Leave and Medical Act. It covers just 5 percent of all companies and only provides for unpaid leave (up to twelve months) for new parents. Compared to the situation in industrialized European countries, that's pitiful. In France, for example, new mothers are guaranteed four months of paid leave at 84 percent of earnings. Also in France, about a third of all children attend public day-care programs, for which parents pay on a sliding scale according to income. Here, all too often, day-care centers are poorly run or beyond the financial means of those who need them the most.

American business, meanwhile, habitually rewards workers who log double-digit hours and quintuple-digit frequent-flier miles and are available to the company at any time, day or night. What they don't say, or even seem to realize, is that all this dedication comes at the expense of the family. Every hour behind a desk is an hour not at home. Working mothers and fathers who take their responsibilities as parents seriously and thus are not always available to burn the midnight oil face the specter of the "Mommy Track" and the "Daddy Track." These are cute names for a depressing and very real phenomenon: the fact that those workers "saddled" with family duties do not climb as rapidly or ultimately as high on the corporate ladder. Even vacation policy is relevant here. What is a vacation, after all, if not a chance for a parent to spend some unhurried time with his or her family? European business recognizes this and as a matter of course expects its workers to take off a month or more in the summer. In the United States, by contrast, the standard is a miserly two or three weeks, spread out across the entire year.

I don't mean to blame everything on institutions: The American people themselves have a lot to answer for. Of the *Wall Street Journal* poll respondents who said that family breakdown was one of the major problems in the country today, how many see to it that each week they clear aside a significant amount of time in their busy schedules (*everybody's* schedule is busy these days) to devote just to their family? How many make it a point to involve themselves in their children's hobbies, athletic events, homework, friendships, problems? How many even make it a point to have, whenever possible, a meaningful daily conversation with their children? (According to research compiled by the Children's Defense Fund, nearly 20 percent of sixth- through twelfth-graders haven't had a ten-minute conversation with at least one of their parents in more than a month.)

When surveyed, Americans habitually assert, in the abstract, that family takes first priority in their lives. But when given real scenarios, the majority place career, financial pursuits, and personal freedom above family obligations.

No, it's clear that there's been entirely too much talk on the family issue and not enough action. So what am I doing *adding* to the talk? Simple. My goal in this book is twofold. First of all, I will

6

provide a description of where the American family is right now—not the ideological, partisan, finger-pointing we are used to, but a clear-headed portrait, based on talks with and readings of experts, as well as my own views. Some of that description, not surprisingly, will be negative. But quite a bit will be positive. While some people see the American family as *declining*, I prefer to see it as *adapting*. Consider these developments—some of them big in scale, others quite small—all of which will be described in more detail in the chapters ahead.

• In Chapter IV, you'll meet Susan and Cherry, a lesbian couple raising two children. This idea will no doubt be shocking to some older or more traditional readers. But I feel safe in saying that there could be no better example of traditional family values—loyalty, love, nurturing, morality, dedication, and fun—than this family. And, make no mistake about it, they *are* a family.

• One of the largest banks in the country has instituted a stunning array of profamily policies, including a $5,000 stipend to any employee to help pay the expenses of adopting a child, regulations to ensure that a new parent returning to the job can work part time for an indefinite period of time—*without* negatively affecting his or her seniority and prospects for advancement—and no fewer than five state-of-the-art on-site day-care centers. You'll read more about this and other business programs in Chapter VIII.

• The U.S. government, through its cooperative extension service, is about to unveil a pilot program whereby parents of grown children will serve as parenting "mentors" to young moms and dads who are just starting out.

• New technology, often targeted as an enemy of traditional values, is actually serving to bring families closer together. An example is the growing trend of telecommuting, which can enable some parents to work at home instead of being away ten or more hours a day. Another is E-mail, which has enabled and encouraged the members of many far-dispersed families—most of whom would never *dream* of putting pen to paper to write a letter—to stay in touch with each other. Anyone trolling through the Internet, meanwhile, will find (among other gems) FatherNet, a directory of electronic resources designed to help dads in need of guidance.

• The two-career family—another favorite bogeyman—for all the stress it has admittedly engendered, is bringing the generations together, too. Just a few weeks ago, I met an employee at *Life* magazine, who told me that both his parents *and* his in-laws had moved their homes hundreds of miles just to be closer to their grandchildren.

• A hospital in Toms River, New Jersey, on its own and without any government funding, has instituted a "family center" designed to provide a broad range of services to the community: parenting classes, mothers' discussion groups, a twenty-four-hour family hot line, school programs about violence and substance abuse and teen pregnancy, even the providing of car seats to those in need.

Indeed, there are a host of innovative, exciting, and sometimes even heroic people, programs, and ideas out there, already up and running. They will lay the groundwork for the second part of the book: a blueprint of what *more* can be done to help, bolster, and fix the American family as we approach the year 2000.

So let's get on with it. There are only a few more years to go!

PART 1

The Family Today . . .

CHAPTER I

What Is a Family?
A Personal Perspective

The question that begins this chapter may seem like a real humdinger but, given that the debate about the family is, underneath it all, a debate about definitions, I really couldn't avoid it.

And almost everybody does have a definition. The sociologists, of course, have one perspective. According to *A Dictionary of the Social Sciences*, "The human family may be defined as an institutionalized bio-social group made up of adults (at least two of which, unrelated by blood and of the opposite sex, are married), and children, the offspring of the maritally related adults; the minimal functions of which are the providing of satisfactions and control of affectional needs, including sexual relations, and the provision of a sociocultural situation for the procreation, care, and socialization of offspring."

As broad as that definition is, many people would find it unacceptable. Gays and lesbians, of course, would object to the phrase "of the opposite sex." Single parents and stepparents and childless couples would want to know why *they* were excluded. And social conservatives would pitch a fit when they read "*at least* two of which . . . are married." For them, a family is one husband and one wife, preferably with children; no one else (except possibly widows and widowers) need apply.

At the other end of the scale, a still broader—and very modern—definition of family was offered not long ago by the *Journal of Home Economics*: "The family is a unit of intimate, transacting and interdependent persons who share some values and goals, responsibility for decisions and resources, and have a commitment to each other over time." "Over time" and not "forever"!

What neither definition recognizes, interestingly, is the idea of extended family. This doesn't just mean uncles and grandfathers and cousins living under the same roof, but the sense of being connected in a strong and irreplaceable way to past and future generations, to ancestors and descendants. To my mind, this is one of the *most* important qualities of family, but it has always been less recognized in the United States, that bastion of individualism, than in most other countries of the world.

Of course, the notion of what a family is and the significance it has is an important—indeed, a defining—issue for every culture. At the very least, a species—human or animal—needs a way to ensure that its young are nurtured during the period of time before they can fend for themselves. What separates human beings from animals is that we go beyond procreation and minimal care and construct families into intricate, clearly defined, and powerful social organizations. Every culture has a different conception of the family: It can be patrilineal or matrilineal, allow for polygamy or require monogamy, worship ancestors or idealize the young, stress the extended family or concentrate on the nuclear unit. And to us, some of these notions seem strange, even bizarre. In the Trobriand Islands, for example, the closest bond a man can have is with his sisters' sons, rather than his own, who are considered part of his wife's family. A native group in southern Mexico does not even have a word to indicate a "family" of parents and children; the key social unit in their culture is the "house."

Except for a prohibition against incest, which is virtually universal, the only thing common to all cultures' views of kinship and the family is that those views are absolutely central to that culture. And woe to the individual who defies them. Recently I was talking to a taxi driver who was a Muslim, originally from Pakistan. He was the only one of thirteen children who didn't marry a spouse chosen by the parents; instead, he married an American girl he met while studying in this country. Even though he visits home every year, even though his wife converted and his daughters are being raised as Muslims—still, because of his defiance of the traditional view of family, his father refuses to speak to him. (He does, however, deign to speak to the little girls.) I asked my driver how long he thought this tradition will continue. He said, "At least one hundred years."

In literature, too, family is an omnipresent theme. As Tolstoy wrote in the first lines of *Anna Karenina*, "Happy families are all alike; every unhappy family is unhappy in its own way." While this is hyperbole (I know "happy" families that have absolutely nothing in common), it is true that conflicted, dysfunctional, or outright warring families offer the writer a richer literary vein to mine. They have sometimes brought writers to a pitch of fury—like André Gide, who wrote, "Families, I hate you! Shut-in homes, closed doors, jealous possessions of happiness." And they have sometimes inspired them to write masterpieces. Greek tragedy (where do you think the term "Oedipus complex" came from?), the Bible (there has never been a more riveting story of sibling rivalry than that of Jacob and Esau), *Hamlet, Pride and Prejudice, David Copperfield, Huckleberry Finn, The Three Sisters, Remembrance of Things Past, To the Lighthouse, Ulysses, Long Day's Journey into Night, Death of a Salesman, The Glass Menagerie, Portnoy's Complaint, The Color Purple, Dinner at the Homesick Restaurant,* even *Gone with the Wind.* It's hard to think of a major literary work that's *not* to a significant degree about family.

In each of the major religions of the world, a central importance is attached to family. I'm most familiar with Judaism, and in it family is perhaps the strongest value there is. The family in the Bible was called *bet av,* or house of father, which gives a clue to the fact that the traditional Jewish family is patriarchal, with the father wielding almost supreme authority. (Remember that Abraham was about to sacrifice his own son, and could have done so with impunity.) A man could divorce a wife, but not the other way around. Fertility was so honored, and barrenness so abhorred, that an infertile woman was permitted to employ another woman to carry and bear children for her. Mitigating some of this harshness was the emphasis placed on children and domestic harmony. As a commentator once wrote, "A man should strive to spend less than his means on food, up to his means on clothes, beyond his means on honoring his wife and children because they are dependent on him." The holidays and rituals of the year were—and are—themselves family events, occasions for shared worshiping, celebrating, and togetherness.

In Islam, too, the family is supremely important. The Koran's characterization of the relationship between husband and wife—"They are a garment to you and you are a garment to them"—is a poetic depiction of the closeness, protection, and comfort the marriage bond ideally should provide. I should note that the Muslim view of marriage also includes a decided inequality in the power balance between men and women. As the Koran says, "Men are the protectors and maintainers of women, because Allah has given the one more strength than the other, and because they support them from their means. Therefore righteous women are devotedly obedient."

In Catholicism, key notions about family include the importance of chastity outside of marriage, the equality of the sexes before God, the value of human life, and the indissolubility of the marriage bond. Its doctrine holds that only a family founded on a permanent and exclusive union can provide an environment for mature love and for the nurturing of children. In 1994, the International Year of the Family, Pope John Paul II issued a statement that the family "is not an institution that can be modified at will: The family belongs to humanity's most fundamental and sacred heritage! It even has priority over the state, which is obliged to recognize it and has the duty to protect it on the basis of clearly understandable ethical and social actions that can never be neglected."

Among members of the Church of Jesus Christ of Latter-Day Saints—otherwise known as Mormons—the family is the basic unit of life, an extension of the family of God and the only human social organization intended to continue into the next life. Indeed, earthly families can expect to live again as extended families with ancestors and descendants who have died. And because of this glorification of the family, Mormons tend to have *large* families: While polygamy is no longer officially permitted, the Mormon stronghold of Utah still has the highest fertility rate of any state in the Union. While I personally don't agree with every tenet of the Mormon faith, I applaud their emphasis on family. I especially like their custom of designating one night a week Family Night. Each week, one member of the family gets to choose an activity—it could be playing softball, or cooking a meal, or just watching a (G-rated, I'm sure) video—and everyone else is required to participate.

In looking at the ways American ideas of family differ from those found elsewhere, the most striking area of contrast has to do with extended family. In most cultures throughout the world, past and present, there was and is much less emphasis on the nuclear family of mother, father, and child that has by and large been the focal point of the family in the United States. Instead, several generations habitually live under one roof—and sometimes uncles, aunts, cousins, and in-laws, as well. In some cultures—the Israeli kibbutz is a prominent example—there are large communal "families" whose members aren't even related to each other. Here, it's not just that extended families don't live together; very often, the members don't even live in the same time zone and, in too many cases, they just aren't important presences in others' lives.

Ironically, we in the United States have broken loose from the nuclear family over the past few decades, but in an unprecedented way: The new extended family is a product of divorce. A child's family can now consist of her biological parents, a stepfather and stepbrothers, her father's new wife, and two sets of grandparents, aunts, uncles, and cousins! (And all bets are off if one parent, or both parents, gets a second divorce and a third spouse.)

Another somewhat backhanded way we are moving toward a new kind of extended family has to do with economics. Only a few decades ago, it was frowned on if a child came back to live at home after college. Now more and more young people are doing it, in large part because they cannot afford to live on their own. At the same time, with the graying of the population, I predict that more middle-aged people will start to take in their elderly parents, in a return to the extended family of yore.

One thing is true in both the United States and the rest of the industrialized world: Over the past few centuries, the family has abdicated many of its functions to the state or to other institutions. In the preindustrial era, virtually everything with respect to children was the responsibility of the family: religious and intellectual schooling, socialization (or training in the ways or beliefs of the culture), safety and security, recreation, nurturance, and sustenance. Today it's only the last two—the financial and emotional functions—that are taken care of at home. (And even they are being eroded by such diverse phenomena as welfare, nannies, and large purple dinosaurs.) A whole host of social entities—from churches and synagogues to schools to video arcades to the police to Little League and Girl Scouts—attend to the rest. Incidentally, I don't think it's a coincidence that our current obsession with talking about and worrying about the family has come to pass just at the moment when the family has been stripped of so many of its former duties. It may just be that, subconsciously, our social discourse is taking note of and protesting that fact.

As for me, I'm not being immodest when I say I have a unique perspective on family, as I think you'll agree when you read about the different family situations I have both lived in and studied. In fact, if anyone has experienced more different kinds of families than I, I would love to hear from you! I guarantee we would have a fascinating conversation.

I grew up in a solidly middle-class, religious Jewish family in Frankfurt, Germany. My father's family was middle class, that is; my mother was a household helper who had come from the country town of Wiesenfeld to live in his house. Ironically enough (given that I was to become famous as an advocate of it) my parents didn't use contraception at the appropriate time, and they were married shortly after realizing that my mother was pregnant.

We spent every summer until I was ten in Wiesenfeld, and it was there that I experienced some of my happiest memories. I was my maternal grandparents' first grandchild (my mother was the oldest of six children), which was no doubt why I was a little bit spoiled. I loved being with my mother's siblings, especially her brother Benno, who worked with his father on the farm, and her youngest sister, Ida, who was only a few years older than I and whom I, as an only child, looked on as an unofficial big sister.

In Frankfurt, my paternal grandmother, my parents, and I lived in a crowded four-room apartment. I have almost all happy memories of my time in Frankfurt, too, and again I think much of it was that I was spoiled, as only an only child can be. A lot of my favorite memories have to do with food. We didn't have an oven, so my mother would knead dough, then send me with it to the baker, who would bake it for us. Every Friday afternoon she would send me with two loaves of challah, plus a little one for me. She also made cakes with streusel on top, little sweet crumbs, and I used to pick some of them off on the way home, carefully choosing pieces that wouldn't be missed.

I think I inherited my talkativeness from my grandmother Selma, who was a wonderful presence in my life. Every Sunday she would take me to a park called the Palmengarten, where she met with her sister Regina and her friends, all of whom had brought along their grandchildren. We would always eat *Baiser mit Schlagsahne*, a delicious white pastry.

I suppose I dwell on those happy times because the next stage of my life was so terrible. I was born in 1928. In 1933 Adolf Hitler was named chancellor, and that year Jews were forced out of government service and universities and barred from entering the professions. The Nürnberg laws of 1935 deprived Jews of virtually all human rights—including the right to marry persons of German blood. And in November 1938 came Kristallnacht, when horrible excesses against Jews were committed all over Germany. Our synagogue was burned down and my school was closed. A week later, the SS came to our apartment and took my father away to a detention camp.

As bad as things were, it was clear they would only get worse.

17

Through a stroke of luck, my mother and grandmother were able to arrange for me to be transported to a children's home in Switzerland that had been set up to house 300 German-Jewish children who were orphans or whose fathers were in a camp. And so, in January 1939, my mother and grandmother put me on a train to Switzerland. I never saw them—or my father—again.

The home was in a rustic setting, in the mountain town of Heiden, near the German border. But the physical beauty belied our unhappiness at having been taken from our homes and having left our families in such uncertainty and peril. Our one saving grace was that we children had each other. In a way, we functioned as our own support system. We were as close as brothers and sisters, and in some cases closer, because there was no question of sibling rivalry over parental preferences; we all got exactly the same treatment, and we knew it.

Not surprisingly, I've stayed close with many of the children from the home—even though it's been over half a century since we met, and even though our respective travels have taken us all over the globe. I recently spoke to one of these people, Marga Miller, about our time there, and she remembered, "There was no jealousy. We had a very hard time and we were all in the same situation. Before I came to the home, I was in a foster family in Switzerland, and even though psychology says that it's better to be in a family, I felt better off in the home. In a family, I was only with myself, but when I came to the home, all the kids were in the same boat."*

One of the positive aspects of the home was the discovery that I liked being with younger children, and from the start I helped out with them; they were like the brothers and sisters I never had. When I was ten, I was responsible for a boy who was six. (He's now a professor in Haifa.) Later I was put in charge of a group of little Boy Scouts; I'd take them hiking and swimming. Soon I came to the

---

*An interesting comment, especially when you consider it in light of recent proposals that the country make a major commitment to building and organizing orphanages. I don't like the word *orphanage*—and I would *never* advocate taking a child away from his or her parent except in the most extreme circumstances—but I do think that it's worth considering when the alternative is foster care, which has been shown to have many problems of its own.

decision that I should use this interest professionally and become a kindergarten teacher.

For the first couple of years I was in Heiden, I received letters from my parents. (My father had by then been sent home from the labor camp.) Then the letters suddenly stopped. By the time the war was over, in 1945, it was clear that they and the rest of my relatives had been killed in what would later be called the Holocaust. But as clear as it was, I didn't come to terms with the truth for decades. In the 1960s, I did some short-term psychotherapy, and after I described my background in the first interview, the therapist said, "So, you're an orphan." I was shocked. Until that day I had never thought of myself in those terms.

But, back in 1945, I did know that I had to decide where to go. Returning to Germany was unthinkable, and Switzerland had made it clear that they did not want us. In order to go to another Western European country, you had to have a relative already there, which I didn't. As for the United States, at that time it was like a fantasy straight out of a Shirley Temple movie.

The answer, for me, was Palestine (soon to become Israel), where many of the surviving Jews of Europe would emigrate after the war, hoping to build a new life—and a Zionist homeland. After a difficult passage, I and the others who had come to the same decision made it to Haifa, where we dispersed to different kibbutzim. And it was on the Ayanot kibbutz, near the town of Nahalal, that I had my next experience of family.

The kibbutzim were designed as communal, almost communistic, collectives, where personal property and the importance of the nuclear family were both very much deemphasized. Once a child was born, it stayed with its mother only one month. After that the child went straight to the children's house, where he or she was brought up by nurses and teachers. For the rest of its childhood, the child spent virtually all his or her time in the group; the parents visited two hours a day, from five to seven in the afternoon, and on the Sabbath, and that was it. Part of the reason for this, besides the communal philosophy, was to stress that women were free and equal, without the drudgery of the kitchen and laundry and so forth. But it didn't work out that way. As soon as the child was born, the mother went back to the housework in the communal kitchens or laundry rooms.

And the communal approach to child-raising had a lot of problems, too. At the beginning of Israel's history, the kibbutzim were a necessity, because *every* adult was needed to work, to build the country, and the idea of day care was unheard of. But even at the start there were problems. Children didn't sleep with their parents, and a tremendous jealousy arose between parents and caretakers. Eventually, when the economic necessity no longer existed, the communal child-care arrangement fell apart, and today, it is retained in only a handful of kibbutzim.

On the other hand, while this system lasted, it fostered a tremendous sense of belonging, almost like my experience in the group home. These people literally grew up together, from birth to age eighteen. The kibbutzim instilled self-reliance together with a willingness to be present for others; it's no coincidence that a high proportion of the fighter pilots in the Israeli Air Force have been kibbutzniks. Interestingly, the children brought up together have not tended to marry each other; I guess when you've been sitting on the potty next to each other for years, sexual attraction wanes.

As for me, I continued with my goal of becoming a kindergarten teacher, and I was able to enroll in a seminary in Jerusalem. It was what I had always wanted, but I still had a hunger for what I had been deprived of. I used to walk the streets of the city on Friday nights, look into the windows of all the houses lit with candles and think to myself, They all have families. They all have someone to be with. Why can't I?

My reveries were interrupted by the War of Independence, in which I was an active participant and was even badly wounded in both legs. When it was over, and the country of Israel was established, I got my first job—as a kindergarten teacher to a group of Yemenite children. The Jews of Yemen were being persecuted at that time, and many of them had been flown into Palestine, where they had to adjust to what was essentially a different world. For me, it was yet another exposure to a radically different conception of family. The Yemenite men often had two wives which they had brought from Yemen, one younger and one older; they would get an apartment with one room and a terrace, so that one wife was always out on the terrace and one was inside. At the kindergarten, I felt as if I single-handedly had to bring an ancient people into the modern world. The mother as well as the children came to the school, and I had to teach the mothers many things, including how to give a bath to their kids.

It was at this time that I fell in love and got married. The fact is, I rushed into it—I was only twenty-one—mainly, I now realize, because I so desperately wanted to replace the family I had lost. David's parents were (comparatively) long-time Israelis, having emigrated from Romania when he was three—and they were happy, stable, and financially secure. So, you see, I was marrying his family as much as him. Now there was the possibility of having children (although I was not sure this was physically possible for me, because of my size). Better yet, I could immediately adopt a whole set of ready-made relatives.

David wanted to be a doctor, and shortly after our wedding we moved to Paris, where he would study medicine. (Israel had no medical school at that time.) I got a job as the director of a kindergarten, which I enjoyed, and studied psychology at the Sorbonne—the University of Paris. Getting the chance to observe one more culture was interesting, but unfortunately the marriage did not flourish. After three or four years, we both realized we had married too young, and we divorced.

My next experience of family is one that I've never hidden, but that I've also never wanted to advertise. Like my mother before me, I became pregnant without being married. The father was a handsome Frenchman, and by this time I was living (temporarily, I thought) in New York. We had both gotten jobs at the French embassy and I was studying for a master's in sociology at the New School for Social Research in Greenwich Village. Also like my parents, when we found out that I was going to have a baby, we got married. This was in the 1950s, and I wonder if I would have acted differently if it had been today, when there is less of a stigma on unwed mothers. Probably not.

In any case, I was overjoyed and surprised at the news: I had always feared that I was too small to have children. For three months, I threw up every morning—but with a smile on my face afterward. And when my daughter Miriam was born, and I saw how beautiful she was, I was shocked. It was an amazing, almost transforming experience for me. I thought it was the miracle of the century, that no other woman had ever given birth. My entire life I had been convinced, deep down, that I was unattractive. But when I saw Miriam, my self-image started to change. Once somebody lent me a gorgeous French baby carriage, which was almost as tall as I was. One day I took it all the way from our apartment on the Upper East Side of Manhattan to the New School in the Village—a distance of four miles—just so I could show off Miriam to everyone.

When Miriam was one year old, her father and I separated, and not long after that we divorced. He was good and kind to Miriam, but we both had come to realize that what we had had together was a fabulous love affair and not much more. We had different interests and inclinations, and there was also the issue that I still planned eventually to return to Israel, whereas he wanted to live in Europe.

So there I was, a single mother in New York. It was a difficult but exciting time. I had a job in market research, calling people up on the phone and asking their opinion about one thing or another, but I was still making only about a dollar an hour. With that I had to pay our seventy-five-dollar-a-month rent, clothe us, and feed us. (I was on a scholarship at the New School, and a charitable organization paid for Miriam to go to nursery school during the day.) How did we do it? I'm still not sure. We subsisted on sandwiches and eggs, I *never* had new clothes, I had a large group of very generous friends who helped us out with all sorts of things, and somehow we managed to get by.

The friends were very important. Not only was I an only child, but virtually all my family had been wiped out by the Nazis. The only relatives I had left were an aunt in London, one uncle in Israel, and another in San Francisco. From my own childhood experience of summers on the farm and long talks with my grandmother Selma in Frankfurt, I knew how important an extended family was to a child. So I cultivated from among my friends honorary "aunts" and "uncles" for Miriam, people who would take an interest in her, follow her progress, teach her things about which I had no idea. (I always made sure, of course, that I had their consent before I carried through with this plan. While some people were honored and delighted to be asked to become a part of Miriam's "family," others preferred not to, and I respected their wishes.)

I was determined, too, that our situation wouldn't prevent me from having fun. I didn't have money for baby-sitters, so I would throw parties at our apartment. I provided the room and the potato chips, and the guests brought everything else. When *other* people gave the parties, I would bring Miriam with me. I would put her on the bed where people had piled their coats, clear a little space for her, and she would sleep right through the noise.

So when I hear and read about people who say that living in a single-parent household is disastrous for a child, I have to laugh. There is nothing inherently detrimental about the situation as long as there is plenty of love and—what is maybe just as important—a strong support system in place for the parent. For many people, this support system consists of grandmothers, siblings, and other relatives; for me, it was friends and charitable organizations.

Not surprisingly, the family was the object of my study at the New School: My master's thesis was on the children who were at the Swiss home with me. I had observed from those with whom I was still in touch—and this was confirmed when I began researching the rest of them—that they had, on the whole, turned out remarkably well, with a strikingly high percentage having gone on to achieve a substantial degree of professional success, family stability, and personal contentment. When you considered the difficult, parentless lives we had in the home, this would seem somewhat surprising. What explains it, I concluded, was the crucial importance of early upbringing. We had all come from good, solid, middle-class German-Jewish homes, and the values and love we had gotten there outweighed the unhappiness and disruption we experienced at Heiden.

It was about this time that I met my third (and last) husband, an engineer named Fred Westheimer. Fred and I had a lot of similarities: He is a German Jew (his parents had emigrated to Portugal in 1938, and he was sent to this country five years later), and he is rather short. But we also had a lot of differences—I am impulsive and he is sensible; he likes to stay in and I like to go out; I like to spend money and he likes to save it—which strongly contributed, I think, to our attraction and eventual happiness.

We dated for a few months, and though I felt strongly that this was the man for me, he seemed—like so many of his gender!—reluctant to make a commitment. I think the moment he realized the inevitable was one day when he, Miriam (by now five years old), and I were out driving in his Renault. Miriam said, "If you two get married, is this going to be our car?" Fred almost drove into a ditch.

One of the challenges of the marriage, of course, was that Fred would be a stepfather. And it wasn't just Fred: It was important that all his relatives accept—and, I hoped, come to love—these two new members of the family. I sensed then what I firmly know now: It's very important to prepare everybody for what's to come, not just your own child, but everybody around you. You can't expect that somebody will love a new child coming into the family the same way you would take it for granted that a person would love his or her own child. That love has to come of unpressured goodwill.

The same goes for the relatives. I knew they weren't going to jump up and down with joy that Fred had married this woman with a five-year-old child. But if you're intelligent about it, if you don't push it down their throats, if you imply with your behavior and comments that you know that love and acceptance will not come from one day to the next, you will eventually earn it. It worked for me.

Of course, my situation was less complicated than some because Miriam's biological father wasn't in the picture anymore. When the other spouse is still around, some things are more difficult. There will be jealousy and bad feelings and disputes about visiting arrangements and the way the child is being raised, and the support the natural parent will give in terms of money will have strings attached in terms of emotion. The key point, in my opinion, is for the new family to sit down and say, We are starting a new family. There will be problems. And we can deal with them, as long as we are open and maintain our goodwill.

In my case, things went smoothly. Fred and Miriam had a good relationship from the beginning. After the wedding, I told her, "You can call him Daddy or Freddie, it's up to you." She called him Daddy from that day on. And soon, Fred officially adopted her, so he really was her daddy. Best of all, a year and a half after we were married, I gave birth to our son, Joel.

Even though I had two little children at home, I had no interest in being a stay-at-home housewife. (For one thing, I'm a terrible cook and a worse housekeeper.) Fortunately, Fred did not pressure me to become one, and even when Joel was very small, I worked at part-time jobs. If I hadn't had this outlet for my energy, my creativity, my need for contact with the outside world, I know I would have been very unhappy. And I know *that* would have been disastrous for the rest of my family. So while I have nothing but admiration for women who give up their careers when they have children, I most certainly do not condemn the women who make a different choice. Clearly, they feel their work represents a significant portion of themselves; if they stayed at home, that portion would be erased. What they have to do (together with their husbands, if they are married) is to sit down and figure out how the parents can maintain this important aspect of their identity, but *not* at the expense of the children—whether it's through part-time work, flex time, telecommuting, maternal leave, paternal leave, having a grandmother move in for a year, au pairs, first-rate day care, or some combination thereof. It can be done: Where there's a will, there's a way.

My professional endeavors since then have almost all, in one way or another, had to do with the family. When I was ready to go back to work full time, I directed a Planned Parenthood research project that involved taking the abortion and contraception history of about two thousand black and Puerto Rican women in Harlem, a project that gave me a fascinating insight into the beliefs and practices of cultures very different from my own. This was my entrée into the fascinating world of sex, and my work as a sex therapist, which I started in the late 1970s, obviously relates to family, and not only because without sex there would *be* no families. For every client I have ever had, whatever sexual problem has brought him or her to me is *directly* related to his or her family background or situation. I am not a family therapist, but family dynamics is something I always bear in mind.

Two recent projects that involved my lifelong interest in the family were *Surviving Salvation*, a documentary film for PBS for which I served as executive producer in 1992, and the book it led to, *Surviving Salvation: The Ethiopian Jewish Family in Transition* (New York University Press), which I wrote in collaboration with Dr. Steven Kaplan, the chair of the African Studies Department at Hebrew University in Jerusalem. Both had to do with the approximately forty thousand Ethiopian Jews who emigrated from Africa to Israel between 1980 and 1992, and both focused on the effect this upheaval had on the institution of the family.

One reason the situation fascinated me was that the Ethiopians were willing to follow a dream. I admired these people who had left their belongings behind, picked up and walked through Sudan, all for the idea of going to a strange land called Israel. I couldn't help thinking that if more German Jews had been willing to separate themselves from their belongings and their familiar lives back in the 1930s, so many lives might have been saved.

The Ethiopians' move from a tribal culture to modernity in many ways (but on a much larger scale) paralleled the situation of the Yemenites I had encountered forty years before; in examining it, Steven and I focused on the disruptive effects it had on the family. While the Israeli conception of the family, these days, is not too far from the American one, the Ethiopian Jews came from a culture in which social life was organized around a residential household that included widowed parents, divorced siblings, elderly relatives, various children, and even servants, and the importance of an extended family going back as many as seven generations (thus to marry even a third cousin would be considered a form of incest!). Although some considered the Ethiopians "primitive," I found it fascinating to see family cohesion and loyalty from the sixteenth century—all maintained by oral history. It is a lesson for us "modern" people, who need videocassettes and photo albums and computerized family-tree programs to remember, and who even then don't do such a wonderful job of it. The extended incest taboo was remarkably adaptive as well. I remember the "village idiots" I encountered in Switzerland, poor backward souls who were the victims of inbreeding. Even in the mainstream Jewish tradition, it was for a very long time permissible for an uncle to marry a niece.

Another difference from Israeli culture, which like our own is very child- and youth-centered, is that the Ethiopian Jews respected and honored the aged. (This was another tradition I appreciated, especially at this stage of my life.) Finally, in contrast to the relatively egalitarian Israeli society, the Ethiopian Jewish culture relegated women to subservient roles. In one striking practice, menstruating women had to leave their homes and spend seven days in a small hut at the edge of the village. There are two ways to look at this practice, and the similar one in which women who have had babies are separated from the rest of the tribe for up to eighty days. On the one hand, one could say that the women were being shunned and treated as outcasts. But think of this: During the time in seclusion, they are relieved of all their household duties and they are given a chance for unhurried bonding—in the one case with their newborn babies, in the other, with the other women who are menstruating at the same time. I can only imagine the marathon gossip sessions that go on in those huts. Our society could use such a forum for female community and mutual support.

All these contrasts—aggravated by the absence of traditional forms of mediation, social pressure, and communal support—have caused severe family dislocation, and the fact that the Ethiopian children have naturally much more rapidly adjusted to the new country than their parents has made the intrafamily tension even worse. The culture shock has led in turn to a variety of disturbing phenomena, including marital instability, domestic violence, and suicide. I still feel that the Ethiopian Jews will one day be fully integrated into Israeli society. But—because of the central and radically different places notions of family take in the respective cultures—it will be a long, difficult process.

My own family was extended in 1984, when Miriam married a wonderful young man named Joel Einleger, whom I've come to love as a member of my own family. My feelings for him are especially strong, I think, because like me he's an orphan: Both his parents died many years ago. Besides all his other good qualities, I'll always be grateful to Joel for luring my daughter back to this country. Miriam took the Zionist idealism I taught her seriously, and for six years after college she lived in Israel, working on a kibbutz and then teaching English as a second language. She came back to the United States because of Joel, and now they live ten minutes away from me. (My son Joel, meanwhile, an assistant professor of education at New York University, is engaged to Barbara, an assistant professor of English; she and her parents, brothers, and sister will provide an even more extended family—and one that extends into another country, namely Canada.)

In 1990, Ari was born. My first feeling was a sad one, that my parents never had a chance to see their grandchildren, much less this beautiful great-grandchild. But then happy thoughts took over. I thought of an old Jewish song, "Song for Miriam," which talks about how the blood of the forefathers runs in the next generation: In a real sense, my parents and grandparents were getting new life through Ari. And it's not just symbolism: Their genes, their good qualities of health, intelligence, compassion, were literally in him. I also was struck by the thought that Hitler did not succeed, that the birth of Ari was still more proof of his defeat.

I *love* being a grandmother. From the time he was born I have spent a lot of time with Ari, and I have found that the best times are when we are alone together. I told Miriam and Joel I will babysit anytime they need me—except when he is asleep. When he was still a baby, we all went hiking in the Swiss Alps. I was extremely contented to push the stroller with him in it. I walked very fast, so that the others would not catch up with us and we could be alone. And I took him to Walt Disney World, just the two of us. Mickey Mouse (who Ari thinks is his personal friend) drove us in a convertible through a parade, with marching bands and cheering people. I was asked to make an impression of my hands in wet cement, and after I did I put in his little finger. I was thinking that this was a symbol of what happens from generation to generation: You make an impression, and you hope that it is permanent.

So what is a family? There is, as should be clear by now, no one exclusive definition. Families come in every imaginable shape and size. But try this on and see how it fits: A family is a group of people linked together by some combination of love, commitment, cohabitation, children, bloodlines, memories, and thoughts about the future. It's a matter of connection—with each other, with a shared past and future, and with generations before and since. And it's a matter of responsibility. When you're in a family, you don't need to see each other every day, or even every week, but you need to know, unconditionally, that if necessary, those people will be available to you.

It was never said more eloquently or more movingly than by the anonymous writer of Psalms: "God setteth the solitary in families."

However you define it, family is one of the most precious gifts a human being can be given. And it should never be squandered.

CHAPTER II

The American Family . . .
And How It Got That Way

A snapshot of the American family:

• There are 68.8 million families in the United States.* Almost half of them, 33.9 million, contain children under the age of eighteen. (The remainder includes couples who will never have children, couples who have not yet had children, and families where the children are grown or have left home for other reasons.) Families with children had an average size of 3.19 people (down from 3.58 in 1970), and the average number of children per family is 1.9.

• Among the implications of the reduction in average family size is at least one positive development. Since average family income remained relatively stable over this period, the *average* child—and I stress that this will be of cold comfort to the millions of boys and girls living in poverty—will have greater financial resources at his or her disposal.

---

*In this discussion I have taken almost all statistics from surveys and studies conducted by the United States Census Bureau. The Census defines family as including only those persons living together in a household who are related by birth, marriage, or adoption. This means that a brother and sister who live together would be considered a family, whereas a cohabiting couple (whether heterosexual or homosexual) or an extended family living apart from each other would not. The Census figures are the best—in many cases the only—statistics available, and my use of them does not imply that I accept the definitions they employ.

• More and more households are *not* families. The number of women living alone rose from 7.3 million in 1970 to 14.2 million today, and the number of men living alone increased from 3.5 million to 9.4 million. In all, more than 25 percent of U.S. households consist of just one person; it is the fastest-growing household category throughout the developed world. These single people are of different ages, meaning that the rise in single people is both a result of changing mores (more divorced people, more people who never have married or never will) and the aging population (more widows and widowers). Meanwhile, the number of unmarried couples living together has jumped sevenfold since 1970, from 523,000 to 3.5 million. The median age at first marriage has steadily increased for both men and women since the mid-1950s: from 20.1 to 24 for women and from 22.5 to 26 for men.

• Children's living arrangements are more diverse than they have ever been. Nearly 10 percent of American children do not live in a household headed by at least one of their parents. Of those who do, 70 percent live in two-parent families and 30 percent live in one-parent families—respectively, a 19 percent decrease and a 231 percent increase since 1970. (In the overwhelming majority of cases, the parent who's present is the mother.) Only about 50 percent of two-parent families are of the "traditional" variety, composed solely of biological parents and (if siblings are present) full brothers and/or sisters.

• The change in family composition has been particularly dramatic for black families. In 1970, 64 percent of black children lived with two parents and 36 percent lived with one parent. Today, the figures are almost exactly reversed: 63 percent live with one parent (again, usually the mother), and a mere 37 percent live with two parents.

• The federal government estimates that 61 percent of children born in the year 1987 will spend some time in a single-parent household before they reach the age of eighteen.

Obviously, one cause of these trends is the increase in the divorce rate, which quadrupled in the late sixties and seventies. However, after peaking at 5.3 per 1,000 population in 1981, it has stabilized in recent years, at 4.7 per 1,000 population. The Census Bureau now predicts that four out of ten first marriages will eventually end in divorce, down from past projections of five out of ten first marriages. (For second marriages, the figure is roughly six out of ten.) The median duration of marriage at the time of divorce has hovered around seven years—giving credence to the notion of the seven-year itch. Well over half of all divorcing couples have no children.

Single parenthood is also directly affected by the rise in the out-of-wedlock birthrate, which has tripled over the last quarter-century. Many of those births are to very young mothers; well over half of teenaged mothers have their children out of wedlock. Like the divorce rate in the early eighties, the out-of-wedlock birthrate seems to have stabilized in recent years. In 1992, the most recent year for which statistics are available, it did not increase for the first time in years, remaining at 45.2 births per 1,000 unmarried women. An especially hopeful sign was that the birthrate for young teenagers went down in 1992 (the most recent year for which statistics are available), after having increased for six years in a row.

• Of course, many single parents will eventually marry, and many divorced parents will remarry, which means that family ties are much more complicated nowadays than at any time in the recent past. Nearly 10 million children—or 15 percent of all children—live in "blended" families with a stepparent or half-sibling. Nearly 1 million children live with an adoptive mother and father.

• Fifty-three percent of people aged 18 to 24, and 12 percent of people aged 25 to 34, live with a parent or parents—both figures representing substantial increases. (The 18-to-24-year-old figure includes college students living in dormitories.) Clearly, this is a result of the filling up of the empty nest, the fact that economic circumstances have led more young people, even those with children of their own, to live with their parents. At the same time, due to the longer life expectancies and the graying of the population (in the last two decades, the population aged sixty-five and older has grown twice as fast as the general population), more elderly people—widows, widowers, and couples—are coming to live with their grown children. In all, 7 percent of American children now live with at least one grandparent. (This trend can be expected not only to continue but to accelerate as the baby-boom generation reaches old age.) So the extended family is making a comeback of sorts in this country.

• It has been estimated that there are 1.6 million cohabiting gay and lesbian couples in the United States, and roughly 2 million gay parents (including children born in heterosexual unions before their parent's "coming out" and those born through adoption, cooperative parenting arrangements, or artificial insemination). An estimated 10,000 lesbians have borne children.

• As noted earlier, women have entered the workforce en masse over the past few decades, partly as a result of economic necessity, as real wages have steadily declined in the face of a rising cost of living, and partly as a result of the women's liberation movement, which taught them that they did not *have* to stay at home if they didn't want to. Whatever the cause, this trend has had huge effects on the American family. Of all families with children, only 16 percent—a little over 5 million—fit the traditional *Leave It to Beaver* model, where the father is the only earner and the mother stays home. About 37 percent of married mothers work full time, and another 36 percent work part time. Of all married women with children under six, 59 percent are in the labor force (up from 30 percent in 1970), and of women with children less than a year old, no fewer than 53 percent are in the labor force. And it seems clear that the presence of women in the workforce has had an effect on divorce rates. An unemployed woman who wants to part from her working husband is taking a terrifying step; economically, at least, it is much easier for a woman with a job to do so.

• Not only are there more families where both parents work, but in those families, parents are working more. (In most cases, this was not a matter of choice but of necessity. A recent survey showed that adults in 80 percent of two-parent American families with children worked more hours in 1989 than in 1979, but that their incomes did not rise commensurately. In fact, real hourly pay, adjusted for inflation, fell for husbands in 60 percent of families over the decade; a rise in wives' pay was not enough to make up for it.)

• When it comes to child care, these working families avail themselves of a combination of care in the home by relatives or nannies, day-care centers or nursery schools, in-home care providers and after-school programs. The most popular kind of care—with about 40 percent of mothers of children aged two and under using it—is in a provider's home. The second most popular, with a little over 30 percent using it, is care in the child's home. There are signs that, especially as children get older, the care they are given is inadequate. A recent survey found that 42 percent of children aged nine and under are left home alone at least occasionally. Among school-age children, the Census Bureau reports that 1.6 million children aged fourteen and under—and half a million children aged eleven and under—are left home alone after school every day.

THE FIFTIES FAMILY
IN IMAGE AND REALITY

So there you have it, a snapshot. But snapshots are only useful as far as they go. We look, and we ask, Which beach was this taken at? Who's the man talking animatedly to Aunt Lucy? In the same way, we need to examine just what the foregoing statistics mean; we need context, background, grounds for understanding.

The most dramatic thing that needs explaining is the seeming collapse of the "traditional nuclear family." And the first thing that needs to be said is that the image that comes to mind when we say that phrase isn't so traditional after all. The fact is, at every stage of our history, people have looked back to an idealized family that supposedly existed at some (often uncertain) time in our past and bemoaned its passing from the scene. As historian John Demos has written, "To study the history of the American family is to conduct a rescue mission into the dreamland of our national self-concept. No subject is more clearly bound up with our sense of a difficult present—and our nostalgia for a happier past."

If you had to pick a year when what we think of as the traditional American family was at its zenith, you might choose 1961. After all, the cataclysmic changes of the 1960s were still a wink in Abbie Hoffman's eye; Betty Friedan's *Feminine Mystique*, the book that ushered in the feminist movement, was still just a pile of manuscript papers (it would be published two years later); and *Father Knows Best, Leave It to Beaver, The Donna Reed Show,* and *The Adventures of Ozzie & Harriet* were all still on the air. But consider this passage I came upon when I was browsing around looking at books about the family:

> Gone is the day when an entire family climbed into a wagon or surrey to spend the day together at a picnic, "all day meeting with dinner on the ground," or shopping trip to the county seat. Instead, Johnny goes to the Boy Scouts, Mary to Campfire Girls, father spends leisure time at the Elks Club or corner tavern, mother has her pet charity, bridge club, or goes window shopping. For a time it seemed that radio, TV and automobile might reunite the family, but three radios and two TV sets in every house and two cars in every garage have put an end to that dream.

Those words were published in 1961! Reading them, you can't help being struck by the quaintness of the "modern" reality (Campfire Girls and bridge club) noted by the authors. (Dad's visits to the "corner tavern," on the other hand, have a rather ominous ring in the light of present-day mores.)

But it goes beyond nostalgia: We've traditionally blamed this supposed family collapse for a panorama of social problems. As sociologist Frank Furstenberg, one of the preeminent scholars on the family, has written, "Family historians have been unable to identify a period in America's past when family life was not untroubled. Most are skeptical that the traditional family . . . *ever existed* in the form in which it is sometimes portrayed today: a stable, harmonious, well-functioning, supportive unit in which children were tenderly and skillfully transported into adulthood."

This should not obscure the fact that there *have* been objective changes in the American family over the years. Indeed, the changes have been almost continuous, a fact that in itself gives the lie to a notion that there ever was a "traditional" family. The image that phrase calls to mind—the nuclear family of working father, stay-at-home mother, two to three children, and nobody else living under their roof—in fact has only predominated in one brief historical period, the 1950s (a term that generally refers—and that I will use to refer—to the period from the end of World War II until roughly 1964). And during the fifties, a great many unusual circumstances led to this kind of family structure.

Consider the way that the 1950s family was a "nuclear" island. (Not only did Beaver not live with his grandparents; he didn't even seem to be *aware* of them.) In fact, for most of our history the extended family predominated in this country. In 1880, nearly 71 percent of elderly Americans lived with one or more of their children. That figure dropped somewhat slowly during the first part of the twentieth century, reaching 51.3 percent in 1940, then dropped dramatically. By 1980, it was a mere 16.4 percent. (There are not reliable statistics available for the Colonial and early-nineteenth-century periods, but evidence indicates that the extended family was then even more common. Incidentally, as already noted, there are recent indications that the extended family is on the rise again.) Another common presence in households throughout our history up until the late twentieth century was boarders or friends, an unfamiliar concept today, given our assumptions about the home as sanctuary, but unremarkable in an earlier era.

Moreover, even if people did want to live in nuclear families, for much of our history death deprived them of that opportunity with depressing regularity—in the upper classes as well as the lower. In 1850, only 2 percent of the population lived past 65. By 1900, the average life span had climbed to just 48 years for women and 46 years for men. This meant that by the age of 15, 1 out of every 4 children had experienced the death of at least 1 parent. A sizable number of women's deaths, of course, came during childbirth; in cases where the child lived, he or she would never know a natural mother. Orphans (and some children with one deceased parent) lived in a dizzying array of circumstances: with relatives, with friends, in orphanages or other institutions, and sometimes on their own. Even intact families in harsh economic straits would often send their children to live elsewhere.

Or look at patterns of employment. In the pre-Colonial and Colonial era of our history, the family was just as much an economic unit as a social unit, if not more so. There were rigid expectations of duty and responsibility, and little emphasis on "love." In a primarily agrarian economy, *everyone* is expected to work—husbands, wives, and children. (The reason schools are closed in the summertime is a holdover from the era when children were needed to work in the fields.) Even if a man owned a commercial enterprise, such as a store, the entire family as a matter of course put in long hours. And part of this family economy was that wives were involved in *producing* a broad range of goods: making candles and other household items, weaving and mending clothes, growing vegetables in the garden, in addition to doing household chores, carrying the child-care burden, and preparing food.

Things changed with the arrival of the industrial revolution, as the "breadwinner" model, with the man going out to work and the woman staying home, began to take hold for the first time in the history of Western civilization. (The family remained an economic unit much longer in rural America than in the cities.) Women continued to perform household duties, but the availability of factory-made clothing and processed foods relieved them of some of their traditional duties. But new duties—emotional rather than physical—arose to take their place: Women became the centerpiece of a new ideology of sex roles and the family. As the nineteenth century progressed, the family, with the wife and mother presiding, was given the burden of compensating for the moral defects of the larger society, with its competition, strife, and brutality; it was idealized as a "haven in a heartless world."

But ironically, the cult of domesticity and the seeming glorification of women belied a much more restrictive ideology of gender roles. It was no longer the job of a woman to make her family's socks and candles; now it was her job to make her family comfortable. As one woman (quoted by Arlene Skolnick in her book *Embattled Paradise: The American Family in an Age of Uncertainty*) wrote in 1845, "It is a duty to exclude everything permanently disagreeable from the family, for the home should resemble heaven in happiness as well as love."

In the late 1800s, although working-class women (especially immigrants) frequently worked in factories, shops, or offices, middle-class and upper-class married women stayed home. But this social consensus (a prefiguring of the 1950s) did not last very long. The arrival of the service economy meant the creation of many jobs associated with women: secretaries, salesladies, clerks, and, in some cases, professional positions as well. At the same time, the political sense that women should have equal rights and equal opportunity began to take hold with a growing number of people. One result was the Twentieth Amendment, giving women the right to vote, which was ratified in 1920. Another was that, starting at around the year 1900, the number of women in the workforce (including married women) consistently rose—until the 1950s, when the trend dramatically reversed itself. The same held true for education, as a half-century-long increase in the number of women attending college took a sudden downturn in the fifties.

The same held true, in fact, for a broad array of social indicators. The birthrate (the number of children borne per woman) consistently fell over the course of American history—until the fifties, when it shot up. For a hundred years, the average age of marriage and of parenthood consistently fell—until the fifties, when it shot up. (Although we hear much today about the crisis in teen motherhood, the teenaged birthrate reached its absolute peak in 1957, the contrast being that the great majority of those 1957 teen mothers were married.) The divorce rate consistently rose—until the fifties, when it plummeted.

Some 1950s social and economic trends, on the other hand, were part of a continuum with what had come before: the move to the suburbs, an increase in people living in single-family homes, the burgeoning service economy, the hegemony of the automobile. What it added up to in the fifties was that the American family experienced a sudden throwback to nineteenth-century ideology, mixed in with a very twentieth-century economy.

Why? No one knows for certain, but it's possible to make some educated guesses. By the time the fifties dawned, the country had come out of two decades of national trauma—the worst depression in our history, followed by a long, lonely, and often painful war. (During the war, incidentally, the unprecedented entry of women into the blue-collar workforce—Rosie the Riveter and her sisters—was a threatening prospect to men on their way home from the battlefield.) For years, families had had to double up in housing or move in with parents, making the prospect of a home of one's own, surrounded and protected by a moat of green grass, extremely alluring. Another source of anxiety was the cold war: We were told that there were Communists lurking behind every corner and that at any moment the Russians could wreak massive destruction on us by dropping the Bomb. It makes sense that Americans would want to retreat from the slings and arrows of the public world into a safe and idealized cocoon of appliances and babies and picture windows. Even the architecture of the ranch and split-level postwar houses emphasized these ideals, as private, sex-specific spaces—the den, the sewing room, the closed-off kitchen, even the second story, with its intimations of private lives—were replaced by a one-

or one-and-a-half-story blueprint with an open, eat-in kitchen and the ubiquitous "family room."

At the same time, the 1950s family was made possible by strong outside forces. The economy was booming, with the gross national product rising 250 percent between 1945 and 1960. Wages were keeping pace, helping to make it financially *possible* for families to buy their own house and automobile, for wives to stay at home if they so chose, for families to elect to have more rather than fewer children. Because of low birthrates during the Depression, there was little competition for all the new jobs the expanding economy was creating, and the unemployment rate plummeted. By the mid-fifties, 60 percent of Americans had a middle-class standard of living, compared with only 31 percent in the last year of prosperity *before* the Great Depression.

The good times didn't just happen: They were in large part a product of government policies, some of them intentional, some inadvertent. After the war, private companies reaped the benefits of more than $50 billion worth of government-funded wartime innovation, which helped fuel the boom. Washington paid for the highways that made the new suburbs possible, footing 90 percent of the bill for the construction of some 80,000 miles of roads. And it played a big part in filling these new communities with Cape Cod–style, ranch, and split-level housing. Before the war, banks typically required 50 percent down payments and offered mortgages of only five to ten years; after the war, through the Federal Housing Authority, the government saw to it that home buyers could put down just 5 to 10 percent of the purchase price and pay the balance off over thirty years, thus getting a three-decade, tax-deductible reprieve from inflation. The GI Bill made it even easier for veterans to get mortgages (they only had to put down a dollar), and it paid for their college tuition. In the early fifties, a full 40 percent of men between 20 and 24 qualified for GI benefits. We hear a lot today about the government being too intrusive. Funny that we didn't hear much about it then.

The upshot was that in the fifties, the average thirty-year-old man could buy a median-priced house with just 15 percent of his income. Today, it takes 40 percent.

Family historian John Modell has argued that another government policy, the commitment to a large-scale peacetime draft, also contributed to the high marriage rates and birthrates in the fifties. By marrying and having children, a man could (consciously or not) avoid the draft. Even if he was already in the service, being married meant being eligible to live in an apartment rather than the standard barracks.

One thing that's clear is that people of the time realized that, far from living "traditional" family lives, they were embarking on something completely unprecedented. "The family ideal of that time was *new* and was recognized as such by participants," says historian Stephanie Coontz. "You can see this in the newsreels of the time. There was this idea that you leave your older neighborhoods and communities, your parents and other relatives, and create this new self-sufficient little nuclear family. Part of it was that there had been so much pain in the '30s and '40s, with the Depression and the War; here was a chance to get away from that to a whole new life.

"There was a new notion that the family—the white family, that is—could really be a place where you lived out the good life. And the sitcoms of the time, like *Leave It to Beaver, Ozzie and Harriet* and *Father Knows Best*, showed you how to achieve this idyllic existence. Here's what you do: get a car, buy a ranch house, get some Hotpoint appliances, and move to the suburbs. All these material trappings will make your life happy."

Our idealizing of the 1950s family doesn't just have to do with structure: the working father, the stay-at-home mom, the two kids, the house in the suburbs. It also has to do with *feeling*. We have the sense that these families were stable, functional, happy. As is often the case, the truth is a little more complicated.

While the popular image was that women were pampered and led a life of relative leisure (remember those "window shopping" excursions?), the reality was different. The pressure on the family—

and the family home—to be a perfect little world was really pressure on women. In the nineteenth century, well-to-do women had servants to do the housework; in the fifties, that would have been considered an admission of defeat. And the much-heralded labor-saving devices that promised "less work for mother" often had precisely the opposite result. The vacuum cleaner, for example, single-handedly raised the standard of acceptable cleanliness, thus forcing the housewife to *use* it much more often than her mother (even if her mother had no servants) would have swept. Meanwhile, everyone began to accept the notion, promoted by Dr. Benjamin Spock's *Baby and Child Care* and other parenting bibles of the time, that raising a child was an almost scientific enterprise, that he or she would fail or succeed, be happy or miserable, be "well adjusted" or a delinquent based on the parents' skill and dedication. Historian Glenna Matthews has estimated that child care absorbed no less than twice as much time in the fifties as it had in the twenties. It doesn't take a genius to see who was spending all that time on it (and facing up to all those expectations). With fathers off winning the bread, and nannies not socially acceptable or (in the great majority of cases) economically viable, child care was virtually the sole responsibility of mothers.

Mothers who chose to work for reasons other than economic necessity were viewed as strange or downright pernicious. A 1948 marriage guidebook included a "Test for Neurotic Tendencies," on which women lost points for exhibiting a desire for authority in the workplace. A 1954 *Esquire* article called the phenomenon of working wives a "menace"; *Life* magazine called it a "disease."

It wasn't just women who had to conform in the fifties. *Anyone* who declined to conform to society's standards had hell to pay; more than any other period in our history, the fifties were intolerant of experimentation, individualism, and diversity. The society at large looked askance at childless couples, families who were unconventional in the realms of religion, dress, even diet. And homosexuality was more harshly stigmatized in the fifties than it had been in any time in the previous century. It was officially a mental illness, at least according to mainstream psychiatry. Untold numbers of gays were forced into loveless marriages that led to profound unhappiness for both themselves *and* their spouses.

The overall pressure toward homogeneity led society to ignore or deny the more malignant strains of noncomformity. The major journal of American family sociology did not carry a single article on family violence between 1939 and 1969. Reports of incest, meanwhile, were increasingly defined as female "sex delinquency." In this atmosphere, it is not surprising that what is probably the vast majority of victims did not report what had been done to them, at least not at the time. A particularly striking example was Marilyn Van Derbur, Miss America of 1958, who revealed to *People* magazine in 1991 that between the ages of five and eighteen, she was regularly abused by her "respectable" father. (If people didn't reveal enough about their problems in the fifties, it could be argued that in our therapeutic era, people reveal too much, and to too many people.) It is impossible to say if there was more physical and sexual abuse—or other acute problems, like alcoholism or depression—in the fifties than in other eras. But it seems clear that in the tight-knit prewar urban communities there was a greater chance of a neighbor or relative reporting or at least noticing such situations, which would in itself serve to regulate their incidence. In the nuclear fifties, every family had become a self-regulated island, for good or ill.

A lot of things went on behind those curtained picture windows that were not recognized by the society at large. The teenage birthrate soared, reaching a high in 1957, at 97 per 1,000 population, and has not been equaled since. By contrast, in 1988, the most recent year for which figures are available, 56 out of every 1,000 teenaged girls gave birth. Of course, that number would be higher if abortion weren't as widely available as it is; approximately 46 pregnant teens per 1,000 had abortions in '88. Given that this was essentially not an option in the fifties, it would seem that the overall teen pregnancy rate was roughly the same in 1957 as it was thirty years later.

One key difference between the decades is that many more of those fifties teenaged moms were wives, too. (Of those who weren't, virtually none kept their babies and raised them as single parents; instead, they gave them up for adoption. Between 1944 and 1955, there was an 80 percent increase in the number of out-of-wedlock babies placed for adoption.) But don't be too quick to paint these young mothers and their husbands as standard-bearers of "traditional family values." The fact is that a lot of them *had* to (or felt they had to) get married: The proportion of white brides who were pregnant at the time of marriage more than doubled in the fifties. (Sociologist Frank Furstenberg, only half-jokingly, calls pregnancy "part of our courtship ritual.") No doubt we would see more of this pattern today, if only it were as *economically* feasible for teens to marry as it was in the fifties. Today, far fewer potential husbands earn enough money to support a family.

Sexually, the double standard prevailed. In courtship situations, men were deemed to be single-minded sexual predators, and it was up to women to control them. "Men no longer bore the responsibility of 'saving themselves for marriage,' " writes Stephanie Coontz. "This was now exclusively a woman's job. In sharp contrast to the nineteenth century, when 'oversexed' or demanding men were considered to have serious problems, it was now considered 'normal' or 'natural' for men to be sexually aggressive. The 'average man,' advice writers for women commented indulgently, 'will go as far as you let him go.' " Not surprisingly, being a sexual traffic cop did not always have a beneficial effect on a woman's own sexual response. And after marriage, of course, if she was deemed by her husband to be insufficiently responsive—"frigid," in the unsavory term of the time—it was her fault. (By the way, since this is my area of expertise, I can authoritatively tell you that anyone who thinks all this has completely changed since the fifties is living on Fantasy Island.)

Women were getting mixed signals from everywhere. A 1955 "home manual" counseled, "We no longer say, 'Woman's place is in the home,' because many women have their places outside the home. But the home belongs to the family, and it is still true that the family is woman's chief interest; it is even more a privilege and a trust, whether she has a job or not."

All in all, what could be called the hypocrisy of the fifties—the way unhappiness, "deviance," or frustration so often contradicted the official Ozzie-and-Harriet image, yet could never be publicly recognized or acknowledged—led to a profound ambivalence in the American people, especially women and especially as the postwar period wore on and its hope and expectations were not realized. A 1962 Gallup poll found that 96 percent of American women considered themselves "happy" or "very happy." Yet at the same time, 90 percent of them said they hoped their daughters would get more education than they had, and lead different lives. In 1960, the editors of *Redbook* magazine asked readers to send in examples of "Why Young Mothers Feel Trapped." They received 24,000 replies. Some of the psychological and emotional burdens created by the expectations and strictures of the period can be seen in the development and immediate popularity of tranquilizers. In 1955, there was no such thing; by 1959, annual consumption—almost all of it by women—was 1.15 million pounds. (In some cases the drugs may not have been necessary, but it is significant that doctors saw fit to prescribe them.)

So the fifties family was much more complicated and problematic than it might first appear. For further proof, consider this conundrum at its heart. The children of the fifties were the very same young men and women who came of age in the sixties and, rebelling against the strictures, contradictions, hypocrisies, and social injustices they had been brought up under, spearheaded a social revolution whose reverberations are still being felt. Does this speak ill or well of the fifties family? For social conservatives, who blame the sixties for everything that's gone wrong in America since, it would seemingly speak ill—yet they idealize the fifties family as the best thing since sliced (white) bread. For liberals, who glorify the sixties as a time of honor and virtue, it would presumably speak well—yet they denigrate the fifties family as the height of hypocrisy and repression. The paradox is evidence of the fact that the fifties family is still very much a matter of image rather than reality.

To complicate matters further, even to the extent that the fifties were the "Happy Days" (as a nostalgic seventies sitcom put it), they were only happy for a certain segment of the population—basically, nonrural, middle- and upper-class whites. "While government subsidized suburban housing and middle-class social mobility of the 1950s and 1960s," Stephanie Coontz writes, "it promoted a rigid private enterprise system for the inner cities, the poor in general, and blacks in particular—with disastrous results. While the general public paid for roads that suburban commuters used to get home, the streetcars and trolleys that served existing urban and poor areas received no tax revenues, steadily deteriorating in consequence. Similarly, government sewer and water aid projects allocated much more for new construction than for repair, thus favoring suburban expansion over urban renovation. Federal housing support for suburbia exacerbated segregation and decay in the urban ghettoes, as FHA redlining practices systematized previously informal and local racial discrimination in housing. Entire urban areas were declared ineligible for loans, while new federal mortgage institutions such as Fannie Mae and Ginny Mae made it possible for urban banks to divert local depositors' funds to suburban developments all across the country."

In all, 25 percent of the American people—totaling up to 50 million citizens—were poor in the fifties. Among blacks—both one-parent and two-parent families—the poverty rate was 50 percent. Since this was in the days before food stamps, Medicaid, and other social programs, the poverty was in many cases devastating.

Interestingly, at the time, many of *The Cracks in the Picture Window* (as the title of the book of the period put it) were a matter of public concern and debate. Later decades have taken their image of fifties life almost exclusively from the glowing advertisements and situation comedies (which were subsidized, of course, by advertisements). But many other expressions of the times, be they novels (*The Man in the Gray Flannel Suit*), plays

(Arthur Miller's *Death of a Salesman* and Edward Albee's *Who's Afraid of Virginia Woolf?*), social commentary (David Riesman's *The Lonely Crowd*, William H. Whyte's *The Organization Man*, and Dwight Macdonald's scathing critique of middlebrow culture, *Masscult and Midcult*), poetry (the iconoclasm of the Beats), popular song (Tom Lehrer's "Ticky Tacky Boxes"), or the comedy of Lenny Bruce, Mort Sahl, and *Mad* magazine, were critical, sometimes devastatingly so, about the conformity, hypocrisy, and suffocating blandness of middle-class life. "Each suburban family," wrote a critic of the time, "is somehow a broken home, consisting of a father who appears as an overnight guest, a put-upon housewife with too much to do, and children necessarily brought up in a kind of communism."

THE STORY TILL NOW:
WHAT'S HAPPENED SINCE THE FIFTIES

So it's clear that the 1950s American family, far from being the prototype of tradition, was in truth a kind of aberration. But having said that, I should also hasten to point out that, while some of what's happened since then—the drop in birthrates, the rise in average age at first marriage—is a simple falling back in line with long-term trends, other developments are truly revolutionary. The changes that have taken place in the American family (and in other aspects of society as well) over the last thirty years could not have been foreseen—and weren't. In 1962, just before the cultural earthquake, *Look* magazine attempted to look a quarter-century into the future and predict what life would be like in 1987. Although many scientists and other eminent experts were consulted, the results ended up looking a lot like a popular television show of the time, *The Jetsons*: lots of high-tech trappings, but the same fundamental social reality underneath. Thus a typical family of the future was described for readers this way:

"Linda runs her home with extreme good taste and manages her children with serene authority. But she does not try to run or manage her husband." And this was what was on the 1987 mother's calendar: "Clothes disposer repairman here. Shop: buy baked ham pills, scotch and soda capsules. Pay radar bill. Have the Whites and Hammonds over for capsules. Take Bob's jet to hangar for grease job. Go to hypnotist for headache therapy."

Probably the biggest surprise is not that there still aren't any baked ham pills (did any of us *really* expect them?) but that the real-life Linda, in all probability, has a job. In the sixties and seventies, the number of women in the labor force rose some 80 percent. Although the conventional wisdom is that this development was a direct result of the women's liberation movement, and though there is some truth to this view, the reality is a good deal more complicated. The fact is, the return of women to the workplace *preceded* the women's movement. As is usually the case, there were strong economic reasons for this development. One obvious way to maintain a relatively high living standard in the face of a developing economic insecurity was the two-paycheck solution: for the wife to get a job. Many, if not most, of these women were baby boomers, and they were discovering an uncomfortable irony: Born in an age of economic abundance and raised to expect a continually improving standard of living, they entered the job market to find that, precisely because there were so many of them, well-paying jobs were very hard to come by. Moreover, whatever one earned, inflation steadily ate away at it. But it was not until the mid-1970s, when inflation surpassed double-digit levels and even maintaining real purchasing power became a near impossible task, that mothers of young children began taking jobs en masse.

In addition, more women were beginning to look for work after their children left home. This made perfect sense, considering the fact that so many of these baby-boom moms had started bearing children so young, and had their kids so close together, and that life expectancy had increased so substantially. There you were, in your forties, with at least another three productive decades to live, and the occupation you had devoted most of your adult energies to—child-rearing—was over. What else was there to do besides go to work?

And the entry of women into the workplace was a social movement that fed on itself. As women tasted the financial independence that a paycheck helped bring, and experienced the feelings of satisfaction, accomplishment, and camaraderie associated with employment, they naturally were loath to give it all up. At the same time, the barriers they experienced in terms of salary discrimination, "pin collar" pigeonholing, "glass ceilings" blocking opportunities for advancement, and sexual harassment made them all the more determined not to retreat from the battlefield the workplace often seemed to be.

The women's movement is also frequently, if not universally, held responsible for the skyrocketing divorce rates of the sixties and seventies. The movement, so the argument goes, while it had many laudable goals (equal pay for equal work), encouraged, even almost goaded, women to inspect their lives for any possible grievances, and then to act on them, even at the expense of their families. So we had the cultural stereotype of the "angry housewife," as seen in the part played by Meryl Streep in the film *Kramer vs. Kramer*, ditching husband and son and setting off to find herself. (The stereotype was even more satisfying if, like the character played by Streep in another film, *Manhattan*, the woman discovers that she is a lesbian.)

Again, the reality is more complicated. To understand it, one needs to back up a bit. In many traditional societies, divorce is fairly common. In the Muslim world, through a process called repudiation, a man or woman may disown the marriage, after which the woman and her property are transferred back to her family. In the Orthodox Jewish tradition, a divorce, although it is considered regrettable, can be obtained through mutual consent of husband and wife. During the early Christian era, the view developed that marriage was a religious sacrament, and therefore could not be dissolved. Although the United States was established for the most part by Protestants, who didn't subscribe to the marriage-as-sacrament view, divorce continued to be stigmatized for most of this country's history, an attitude undoubtedly related to our long-standing idealization of marriage and the family. (Divorce meant admitting failure in the most important thing in life, and people would rather live in misery than do so.) This stigma lasted up until—you guessed it—the fifties, when the term "broken home" was still used to refer to a family where a divorce had taken place and when the presidential candidacy of Adlai Stevenson was unquestionably hurt by the fact that he had a divorce in his past. (By contrast, twenty years later Americans barely noticed that Ronald Reagan had been divorced, and paid the fact absolutely no attention when they cast their ballots.)

The divorce rate began to rise in the early 1960s—in other words, before the onset of feminism. Economic factors, once again, were at play. In the early American model of family, divorce was close to unthinkable: The family was an economic unit, and the loss of any of its component parts would have spelled disaster. In the "breadwinner" model, lasting into the early 1960s, women were tethered to unhappy, if not downright miserable, marriages by economic necessity; to strike out on their own, in many cases with children to care for, would have seemed foolhardy. When they started to enter the workforce and earn a wage on their own, even a modest one, their options opened up and they began to act on them. And that is precisely when the divorce rate began to rise. This was also the time when all those child brides of the postwar era were beginning to see their children—to whom they had devoted the lion's share of their physical and emotional energy over two decades—start to leave home. All of a sudden, they were alone in the house with their husbands. And sometimes they didn't like what they saw.

Although the divorce explosion of the sixties and seventies—and the fact that the United States continues to have the highest divorce rate in the world—is often painted as a repudiation of "traditional family values," in a significant way it is actually evidence of the *strength* of those values. Polls and surveys historically and consistently reveal that Americans of all ages and backgrounds believe in marriage and strongly desire a happy marriage for themselves; and when things do not work out as well as they think they should, many are unwilling to "settle" for less than the utmost. When there are no children involved—either because none have been born yet or because they have grown up and left the nest—the marriage bonds become even more subject to an invisible happiness barometer, and even more fragile. "Marriage has become a choice rather than a necessity," write family sociologists Andrew Cherlin and Frank Furstenberg, "a one-dimensional institution sustained almost exclusively by emotional satisfaction, and difficult to sustain in its absence."

Americans, both male and female—did not *want* to be tied to unhappy domestic situations, and government institutions recognized and responded to this feeling. Starting with California in 1969 and ending with South Dakota in 1985, every state in the Union enacted laws that allow couples to request a divorce simply because of the breakdown of the marriage. It is currently easier and quicker to get divorced in the United States than it is in any Western country except Sweden. Here, the average waiting period for a divorce decree is one year. In England it is five years and in France it's six.

The third and final familial earthquake over the last thirty years involves out-of-wedlock—what used to be called "illegitimate"—births. By whatever measure you choose to employ, they have skyrocketed. In 1970, there were some 400,000 total births to unmarried women; in 1991, there were more than 1.2 million. In 1970, they represented 11 percent of all births; in 1991, they represented 30 percent. Although single motherhood is accurately perceived to be more common among blacks than whites, it actually has risen more dramatically for Caucasians: from 6 percent to 22 percent of all births for whites in the 1970–1991 time period, as compared to a jump from 38 percent to 68 percent of all births for blacks. Fueling these statistics is the fact that, since 1960, the age of women at their first marriage and the number of women who *never* marry have both been rising. Both trends increase the population of potential unwed mothers.

This rise in single motherhood is all the more striking in view of two simultaneous developments, one of them medical, the other legal and societal. Given the invention and widespread availability of birth-control pills (and of other forms of contraception) on the one hand and the legalization and relative acceptance of abortion on the other, you would think that the out-of-wedlock birthrate would have *fallen*. The fact that the opposite has occurred is explained partly by the fact that there is still widespread ignorance and resistance to birth control, and that many women still do not consider abortion an option. But this is by no means the whole story.

While it is true that many of those single mothers are poor, the widely held notion that welfare causes single motherhood has no evidence to support it. At the same time when single motherhood was increasing nearly threefold, from 1972 to 1992, AFDC (Aid to Families with Dependent Children) benefits declined *26 percent*, adjusted for inflation. (The real value of cash assistance plus food stamps to a typical family of four with no other income fell over that time from $10,133 to $7,657, in 1992 dollars.) Moreover, welfare benefits are much lower in the United States than in other Western countries, yet single motherhood is much more common here. Finally, single motherhood has grown among college-educated women, who are not likely to be motivated by the prospect of a welfare check.

Then what *is* the explanation? Sociologist Sara McClanahan points, first, to the growing economic independence of American women. As with divorce, a woman will be much more likely to decide to have a child on her own if she is pulling down a paycheck. And the fact that men's earnings have fallen so dramatically, especially at the lower end of the economic ladder (between 1980 and 1990, men with a high-school degree experienced a 13 percent decline in earnings), has taken away much of the economic benefit of marriage. Put another way, in 1970, female workers earned just 59 percent as much as male workers; by 1990, they earned 74 percent as much. All these trends are much more pronounced in the United States than in other industrialized countries, making it logical that single motherhood should have risen more sharply here.

Another part of the equation is the shift in social and cultural mores since the 1960s. While unmarried sex was by no means a rarity in the fifties, it was not *talked* about, and any by-products—babies, that is—were certainly not acceptable in polite society. The sexual revolution of the sixties and seventies irrevocably changed our notions of what was proper. More and more people had sex without benefit of marriage; unfortunately, too many of them were having it without benefit of contraception. Meanwhile, the rise in the divorce rate was helping take away the onus on single parenthood. Many single pregnant women who decided to have and keep their babies had grown up in families with just one parent and viewed this structure as normal, if not ideal.

In talking about single-parent families, special mention has to be made of the black family. Thirty years ago, Daniel Patrick Moynihan's famous report *The Negro Family: The Case for National Action* described the African-American family as a "tangle of pathology," in large part because of the problems associated with children growing up in mother-centered families. Moynihan's terminology was ill chosen and his interpretations open to debate. For instance, it could be persuasively argued that the black family structure, far from being pathological, is actually quite adaptive, given the conditions that blacks face. But there is no doubt that since 1965 the black family has become even more strongly characterized by single mothers at the helm. I have already mentioned that in 1993, 68 percent of all black women who gave birth were unmarried. The other relevant statistic is that of all black families with children under eighteen, 63 percent contain only one parent (in the overwhelming majority of cases, the mother). The comparable figure for white families is 25 percent.

Greater minds than mine have spent entire scholarly careers trying to explain these trends, so there is little hope that I will do so by the end of this chapter. But let me at least try to suggest some grounds for discussion. For one thing, consider the fact that in the period from roughly 1970 to 1993, when the proportion of black births that were out of wedlock rose about 100 percent, another index rose almost *150* percent. This was the unemployment rate for black males, which went from 5.6 percent to 13.8 percent. The unemployment rate for black male teenagers (not including those in school) stands at 40.2 percent, and for black men aged 20 to 24 at 23 percent. In 1970, the median income for black families was (in 1992 dollars) $18,810—61 percent of white families' $30,903. This was a national disgrace, but the truly disgraceful thing was that by 1992, the gap had widened. The median black family income was $18,660, representing less than 58 percent of whites' $32,368.

Three factors have an impact on the rate of out-of-wedlock births: (1) frequency of sex; (2) use of contraception; and (3) desire or willingness to marry, either before or after pregnancy. In the case of current-day America, (1) and (2) are constants, (1) being high and (2) being rather low. As for (3), anyone who has studied the modern family will tell you that marriage rates will go up when economic prospects are good—look at the fifties. Marriage is a kind of investment in the future, requiring a sense that, even if things aren't so great now, they will get better. Women without much hope, by contrast, can—and often do—view a baby as something positive, a link to love and the future when all other indicators are bleak. So it makes sense that the current harsh, if not hopeless, economic climate for under- or uneducated black urban males of marriage age should correspond to a decrease in the number of black mothers who are married.

In general, black women face an extremely poor "marriage market," to use sociologist William Julius Wilson's phrase. According to the 1990 census, there were 1.88 million fewer black males than black females in the United States, a shortage attributed to their higher infant mortality rate and to the death of high numbers of them due to homicide, accident, drug overdose, and war casualty. In addition, a disproportionate number of black males, though alive, are effectively removed from the marriage market due to military service, institutional confinement, severe economic hardship, and/or serious substance-abuse problems.

As I have said, I don't believe that the availability of welfare benefits is a direct cause of the increase in out-of-wedlock births, black or white. But there is no doubt that if there were no welfare, there would be fewer such births, as more pregnant women would probably choose to have abortions. (Eliminating welfare, I hasten to point out, would also create much *more* suffering and hunger on the part of children and adults. And I also wonder whether the conservative politicians and theorists who advocate sharp curbs on welfare or its outright elimination would *want* to be in the business of encouraging abortion.) Finally, as in the general population, one cannot discount the significance of example. When out-of-wedlock births increase, for whatever reason, the practice gradually becomes more common and acceptable, and when the possibility arises in any individual's case, it is more likely to be chosen as an option.

CHAPTER III

Watching Ourselves: The Family on TV

It is no accident that when then Vice President Dan Quayle made his controversial remarks on the erosion of "family values" in 1992, he chose to do so by critiquing the actions of a character in a television comedy series. Nor was it particularly surprising that there was an outpouring of public grief following the death of Harriet Nelson in 1994, a sense that in playing television's favorite mom in *The Adventures of Ozzie & Harriet* from 1952 to 1966, Nelson in some way embodied American motherhood.

The fact is, in the post–World War II era, there has been one social force that, more than any other, has conducted a sort of free-floating dialogue with the American family, the one influencing, reflecting, and refracting the other. That force is television. It would appear to be a coincidence of technology that television first became widely available in the late forties, the era in which Americans began to be supremely self-conscious about their family lives. But, coincidence or not, television was bound up with the family from the start.

At first, the TV seemed to be merely one more in a long line of mechanical devices (each successive one requiring less work on the part of the consumer) that had provided home entertainment for Americans since the Victorian era: the piano, the *player* piano, the phonograph, the radio. Each was expected, in part, to fulfill a cultural function, as a way in which family values could be acted out and maintained. But none had the impact of the television, and none was deemed as significant a factor in family life. By 1955, television was installed in two-thirds of the nation's homes. By 1960, the average person watched five hours of TV a day.

At the start, notes Lynn Spigel in her excellent book *Make Room for TV: Television and the Family Ideal in Postwar America,* television was "typically welcomed as a catalyst for renewal of domestic values . . . a panacea for the broken homes and hearts of wartime life." Advertisements typically showed Mom and Dad, Sis and Junior, gathered around the glowing television set, as if it were an old-fashioned hearth; one ingenious designer built a television right into the mantelpiece, so the family could watch the TV and the fire simultaneously. (The custom of televising burning Yule logs at Christmastime, started in the fifties, took this comparison to the level of absurdity.) The previous dominant entertainment form, the movies, and the automobile, which was becoming all powerful in postwar culture, both took people *away* from home and in so doing kept families (at least physically) apart. TV, by contrast, in the words of a 1956 study, "has had the effect of keeping the family at home." The television "set"—almost always housed in a "colonial"-style console of dark wood that comfortingly hid its modernistic, technological origins—was a domesticating tool that actually managed to divide up and parcel out the family's time. Mornings and late afternoons belonged to the kids, the middle of the day to mom. Weekend afternoons, with their sports programming, were dad's domain, and evenings were for the whole family. The television even had an influence on domestic architecture, as the "family room" (the term was coined in 1946) became the repository of the TV in postwar houses. You didn't even have to leave the television to eat—not, that is, after the introduction of the TV dinner in 1954.

But already, it was becoming clear that television was no panacea. Social scientists, newspaper critics, philosophers, and just plain Americans had all become aware of its dark side: the way the addictive television glow tended to crowd out old-fashioned conversation and more wholesome amusements, like crafts and reading; the way (especially as it became more common for households to have more than one set) family members retreated to private spaces to watch separate programs; the way those programs seemed to eat up so much of your time, leaving you feeling bleary-eyed, restless, and somehow soiled. The cultural disaffection with television received its most memorable expression in 1961, when the chairman of the FCC, Newton Minow, described TV programming as a "vast cultural wasteland" containing "a procession of game shows, violence, audience participation shows, formula comedies about totally unbelievable families, blood and thunder, mayhem, violence, sadism, murder, western bad men, western good men, private eyes, gangsters, more violence, and cartoons. And, endlessly, commercials—many screaming, cajoling, and offending."

At the same time that television itself was an issue in the discussion about and conduct of American families, television programming, to a remarkable degree, *concerned* itself with the family. Compare it with the movies. You went out to attend them, and what you saw when you got there was also (except for the occasional Andy Hardy serial) far outside your range of experience. Westerns, costume dramas, historical epics, gangster pictures, emotionally charged melodramas, slapstick comedies with Charlie Chaplin or the Marx Brothers, all-singing-all-dancing musicals— the very *point* of a movie, it seemed, was to show audiences something exotic. By contrast, from the very beginning, television tended to the domestic. To be sure, there were variety shows, drama anthologies, and the "blood and thunder" that Minow complained about, but the staple of television programming turned out to be the mild comedy about unextraordinary families—what came to be known as the sitcom.

In part, this was a matter of economics. Costume dramas and musical comedies are labor-intensive, time-consuming, complicated, and *expensive* endeavors; given the sheer volume of programming that the television networks had to turn out, it makes perfect sense that they should have lowered their sights. But I'm convinced that there was more to it than that. In a strange way, people gathered around the electronic hearth liked—and maybe even needed—to watch representations of themselves up on the screen. They weren't exact representations, or mirror images, to be sure; for that, you could see a home movie you shot with your new Kodak. And, it soon became clear, there were certain conventions that needed to be followed. For one thing, the television family programs were almost always comedies, not dramas: Especially in their homes, people didn't like to be threatened or disturbed or confronted too explicitly with uncomfortable truths. But comedy (as Shakespeare and Twain understood) doesn't have to be tame and bland. As Lynn Spigel writes, "It can create multiple, conflicting and oppositional realities within the safe confines of a joke."

Spigel and other critics have identified 1955 as the year when a major change took place in the family sitcom. In the early years, many of the most popular comedies were about working-class families, many of them urban and many of them "ethnic": *Mama* (an adaptation of the play *I Remember Mama*, about Norwegian immigrants, that went on the air in 1949), *The Goldbergs* (1949), *The Life of Riley* (1949), *Amos 'n' Andy* (1951), *Life with Luigi* (1952), and *The Honeymooners* (1952). Some featured well-known performers who played "themselves" (or thinly disguised versions thereof), as in *The Burns and Allen Show* (1950), *The Jack Benny Show* (1950), Danny Thomas's *Make Room for Daddy* (1953), and, of course, *I Love Lucy* (1951). (All of these shows also had ethnic aspects, Burns and Benny being Jewish, Thomas Lebanese, and Desi Arnaz Cuban.) Many of the married couples in them were childless, and, if children were present, they did not tend to be the prime focus of the plots.

Finally, the early shows—especially the two classic series of the era, *The Honeymooners* and *I Love Lucy*—displayed a level of tension, frustration, and sometimes conflict within the family that wouldn't be seen again until the 1970s sitcoms of Norman Lear. Lucy Ricardo's always unsuccessful attempts to find some meaningful occupation other than housewife were a frequent theme, as was Ralph and Alice Kramden's frustration at not being able to leave their boxlike and claustrophobic Brooklyn apartment. (Beneath Ralph's trademark "To the moon, Alice" was an uncomfortable suggestion of domestic abuse that was a reality in many parallel real-life marriages.) Significantly, these themes were very often played out in plots that specifically revolved around television. Between 1951 and 1955, twelve episodes of *I Love Lucy* were about the Ricardos' television or their *appearance* on television. George Burns, playing "George Burns," spied on his wife and neighbors through the use of his private TV screen.

A classic *Honeymooners* episode, "TV or Not TV," is about the Kramdens' momentous decision to purchase a television set. Ralph is pushed to do so by Alice, who complains, "I have lived in this place for fourteen years without a stick of furniture being changed. Not one. I am sick and tired of this. . . . And what do you care about it? You're out all day long. And at night what are you doing? Spending money playing pool, spending money bowling, or paying dues to that crazy lodge you belong to. And I'm here to look at that icebox, that stove, that sink and these four walls. I want to look at Liberace!"

But the set becomes an unwelcome intruder. We see Ralph come home from work to find Alice watching TV. He asks, "Would you mind telling me where my supper is?" "I didn't make it yet," she replies. "I sat down to watch the four o'clock movie and I got so interested I . . . uh, what time is it anyway?" Eventually, Ralph and his friend Ed Norton monopolize the use of the set, and Alice is forced to retreat into the bedroom for peace and quiet.

All those characteristics changed in the middle of the decade. Taking as their lead *The Adventures of Ozzie & Harriet* (an ironic title if there ever was one), we had such programs as *Father Knows Best* (1954), *Leave It to Beaver* (1957), *The Donna Reed Show* (1958), *Dennis the Menace* (1959), *My Three Sons* (1960), *Hazel* (1961), *The Dick Van Dyke Show* (1961), and *The Patty Duke Show* (1963). Any scent of ethnicity was eliminated, as the surnames of the featured families on these shows were Anderson, Cleaver, Stone, Mitchell, Douglas, Baxter, Petrie, and Lane. (*The Dick Van Dyke Show* was loosely based on the life of Carl Reiner, a Jewish writer and performer, and he was originally supposed to play himself. But network executives vetoed him as "too Jewish" to play his own life, and the part was given to the Waspish Dick Van Dyke. Reiner ended up being cast as Rob Petrie's boss, Alan Brady, who was presumably Irish.)

The families on these programs were all middle to upper middle class and lived in two-story Colonial houses in virtually interchangeable suburbs. Perhaps most significant of all, the tensions between husbands (all of whom have professional positions) and wives (all of whom are happy "homemakers") has been eliminated, except for perhaps an occasional amused annoyance that Dad has forgotten to take out the garbage again. Indeed, except for *Dick Van Dyke*, a transitional program, the entire focus of the shows changed to the now ubiquitous children. Again except for *Dick Van Dyke*, we never saw the fathers' workplace, indeed virtually never left the confines of the home (where, intriguingly, television was hardly ever mentioned). As Spigel puts it, "Dealing with generational rather than gender conflicts, they based their dramatic appeal on sibling rivalries and dilemmas of childrearing."

Once again, there were clear economic reasons for the change in focus. Before the midfifties, television had been a regional, largely urban, phenomenon, but afterwards it was a truly mass medium: For all intents and purposes, every evening found the entire nation (give or take a few oddballs) tuning into one of the three networks. So it made sense that the networks (and the sponsors, who, after all, funded the programming) should have wanted the shows to be as bland, and therefore as inoffensive, as humanly possible. This was what was known as "least objectionable programming."

But there were other forces at work, too. Popular culture works in strange ways, and it is surely no coincidence that in the late fifties and early sixties, just as the cracks were starting to appear in the picture window, television's depiction of the family should have been so resolutely, almost insistently, blind to any flaws. It was a form of wishful thinking, really. As critic Ella Taylor writes in her book *Prime-Time Families: Television Culture in Post-War America*:

The powers that be, who decided in the early 1950s to phase out "ethnic" sitcoms such as *Amos 'n' Andy, Life with Luigi* and *The Goldbergs* and replace them with the upper middle-class coziness of *Leave It to Beaver* and *Ozzie and Harriet*, may well have thought they were reproducing the typical American family—if not of the present, then certainly of the near future—just the people their advertisers sought to reach. What they reproduced, in fact, was less the experience of most family lives than a postwar ideology breezily forecasting steady rates of economic growth that would produce sufficient abundance to eliminate the basis for class and ethnic conflict. The "end of ideology" would produce "middle classlessness," a social consensus with the family as the essential building block, integrating the individual into a benevolent social order.

As far as the society at large was concerned, television continued to wear blinders throughout the sixties. Although this was the era of the Civil Rights movement, there was not a single comedy series with a major black character from the demise of *Amos 'n' Andy* in 1953 until the premiere of *Julia*, with Diahann Carroll, in 1968. And although this was the era of spiraling divorce rates, there was not a single series with a divorced main character until Norman Lear's *One Day at a Time* in 1975. (In *The Mary Tyler Moore Show*, which premiered in 1970, Mary Richards was originally supposed to have been a divorcée, but the idea was nixed by network executives.)

Television's treatment of single parenthood makes for an interesting case study. While the overwhelming majority of single parents are divorced women or women who had their children out of wedlock, sixties situation comedies were overflowing with widowers and (somewhat less frequently) widows: *My Three Sons, The Brady Bunch, The Partridge Family, The Andy Griffith Show, The Farmer's Daughter, The Courtship of Eddie's Father,* and the aforementioned *Julia*, who was a widow. (There was also Brian Keith as a kind of uncle/father in *Family Affair*.) The trend even extended into the western, with *Bonanza*. Clearly, television felt that the only way it could touch this highly charged topic was through an extremely indirect route.

The other trend in sixties situation comedy was the introduction of outlandish, often supernatural, plot elements. Thus we had such programs as *The Flintstones* (the Kramdens in the Stone Age), *Mister Ed*, *My Mother the Car*, *The Munsters*, *The Addams Family*, *The Beverly Hillbillies*, and so on. This is partly explained by the fact that, two decades into the television age, programmers were desperately searching for something new. But it also, I believe, reflects the uncertain nature of gender roles and the family. David Bianculli, the television critic for the *New York Daily News* and the author of *Teleliteracy*, points to two of the most successful of these shows, *Bewitched*, which ran from 1964 to 1972, and *I Dream of Jeannie* (1965–1970), as television's simultaneous recognition of and attempt to harness the nascent women's liberation movement.

"They're both cases where women have all the power and are pressured not to employ any of it," Bianculli says. "Here was Barbara Eden, in the middle of the women's lib movement, running around calling Larry Hagman 'Master.' And on *Bewitched*, Samantha was obviously smarter than Darren. She was always able to come up with a better solution than his to the problem of the week, but he didn't let her use it. The ultimate proof of that was that no one noticed when Dick Sargent replaced Dick York in the part. The moral of that story is, 'One Dick is as good as another.' "

The television nuclear family finally did explode in the seventies, as it could no longer evade the disruptions being experienced in the society at large. The pioneer here was producer Norman Lear. His landmark series, *All in the Family*, which came on the air in 1970, was, on the surface, about two intact nuclear families, those of Archie and Edith Bunker and their daughter and son-in-law, Gloria and Michael Stivic. But the ruptures almost immediately began to appear. The bigoted Archie had nothing but contempt for Michael, whom he called "Meathead," and didn't treat Edith (aka "Dingbat") much better. The typical discourse of the show was a screaming match, as opposed to the well-modulated tones of the sixties family sitcom. And all around the aptly named Bunkers, domestic society seemed to be crumbling. Edith's cousin Amelia's "perfect marriage" ends in divorce. Cousin Maude (soon to have her own series) has been divorced three times. Cousin Liz turns out to be a lesbian. Even Gloria and Michael, after moving to California, separate and divorce. By the end of the show's run, in the late seventies, Edith has died and, Taylor writes, "there no longer exists a nuclear family, only a multiplicity of primary relationships trying to define themselves."

Lear followed *All in the Family* with a series of programs that showed families in various states of distress or collapse: *Sanford and Son* (1972, the first show with an all-black cast since *Amos 'n' Andy*), *Maude* (1972), *Good Times* (1974), *The Jeffersons* (1975), *One Day at a Time* (1975), and *Mary Hartman, Mary Hartman* (1976), about an Ohio housewife "who tried to remain calm [in the words of the encyclopedic *Total Television*] while her daughter was held hostage by a mass murderer, her husband was impotent, her father disappeared, and her best friend was paralyzed." The characters in these shows tried to hold their families and their lives together, but the task often turned out to be too difficult.

Perhaps the most revealing family program of the 1970s was not a comedy but a documentary: *An American Family*, which aired in 1973 and chronicled in twelve episodes the lives of the Louds, an upper-middle-class family in Santa Barbara, California. The Louds were as white-bread, as well-to-do, and as photogenic as the Nelson family, but in every other way they were worlds apart; if the producers wanted to choose a household that emblematized the troubled American family of the seventies, they picked the right one. We soon found out that beneath the surface placidity lay deep and sometimes unresolvable tensions. Much to his parents' horror, Lance Loud turned out to be gay. By the end of the series Pat Loud had decided to file for divorce, and Bill Loud moved out of the house. It is impossible to say how much of the Louds' problems were caused or aggravated—as some commentators speculated—by the presence of cameras in their house. But even their decision to allow the cameras in was revealing of how deeply and irrevocably the notion of family as private sanctuary had unraveled.

The fissures in the nuclear family could no longer be ignored or sloughed off by TV programmers; to have broadcast a program about an intact, stable contemporary family in this period would have been impossible. One tack the networks took was to transplant such clans into the past, thus both feeding into and stoking the nostalgia that had begun to be palpable in the society at large. *The Waltons* (1972) was set in the 1930s, *Little House on the Prairie* (1974) in the 1870s, and the hugely successful *Happy Days* (1974) in the 1950s. In many ways, *Happy Days* was a new version of *Leave It to Beaver*; though he talked tough and wore a leather jacket, Arthur "Fonzie" Fonzarelli was actually a substantially less malevolent figure than the duplicitous Eddie Haskell. Sadly, this benign a view of family and community—with loving parents committed to their marriage, wholesome kids with good values and good employment prospects, and problems that could be solved in twenty-two and a half minutes—could no longer be credibly set in the present day.

And so, for the first time ever, television comedy turned its back on the contemporary family. The landmark program in this regard was *The Mary Tyler Moore Show* (1970), about a single (not divorced) woman for whom the most important aspect of life was her job. The significant thing about *Mary Tyler Moore* was not just that it showed an unmarried woman who was not desperate to get married and who was satisfied with her career; beyond that, it presented work *as* family. Mary Richards, her friends, and her co-workers at WJM-TV constituted a more or less functional clan, with each member playing a well-defined role: Mary was a combination level-headed mother and cherished daughter; her boss Lou Grant was the gruff but caring father; Murray Slaughter and Ted Baxter were, respectively, the sensible and the headstrong sons; and Rhoda Morgenstern was the chatty, comical, and supportive sister. Work was family for all the characters, not just Mary. In addition to Mary, Rhoda and Ted were both single, and the family lives of the married characters, such as Lou, Murray, and Mary's landlady, Phyllis Lindstrom, were not presented as significant; in some cases we never even *saw* their spouses. Mary's tearful remark to her co-workers during the famous last episode of the series in 1977, "You've been a family to me," was redundant: Anyone who had been paying attention already knew that.

The workplace comedy has proved to be a genre of unprecedented staying power, as *The Mary Tyler Moore Show*'s descendants, all employing the same basic formula of a group of unrelated people coming together in an ersatz family, continue to this day. In swift succession we have seen *M*A*S*H* (1972), *Welcome Back, Kotter* (1973), *Barney Miller* (1975), *Alice* (1976), *WKRP in Cincinnati* (1978), *Taxi* (1978), *Cheers* (1982), *Night Court* (1984), *Designing Women* (1986), *Wings* (1990), our old friend *Murphy Brown* (1988), and *Seinfeld* (1990), to name only the most successful. (The same elements were also in place in—and help explain the appeal of—such dramatic series as *Star Trek, Lou Grant, Hill Street Blues, Cagney & Lacey,* and *St. Elsewhere.*) Their popularity showed that, even in an era of seeming family breakdown, Americans still wanted to see images of people who cared strongly about and were *connected* to each other.

By the early eighties, with the success of these programs and of such new genres as the nighttime soap opera, the family comedy was considered dead. Then along came Bill Cosby. The immensely successful *The Cosby Show* (1984) was about a loving, two-parent, upper-middle-class family where father, once again, knew best and where every manner of problem could be solved by the end of the half-hour. In a bow to contemporary mores, Clair Huxtable worked as a lawyer (although her ability to hold that demanding job and manage a large household, without full-time help and without displaying stress, was rather unrealistic, to say the least). Bill Cosby, who produced the show, and whose doctorate in education was prominently displayed in the closing credits, explicitly saw the program as an educational opportunity, as a way to teach, through example and humor, that the family didn't have to be an emotional land mine, that it could still be a place of love, respect, cooperation, and commitment.

These intentions were laudable, but it is no coincidence that *The Cosby Show* achieved its great popularity during the Reagan years, when a culture of highly selective nostalgia overtook the land. This was a time when the family—and especially the black family—faced enormous cultural and economic pressure, yet virtually its only representation on television seemed to live in a protective and expensively furnished cocoon. A more recent number-one series, *Home Improvement* (1992), seems to feed into the same kind of wish fulfillment, with Tim Allen's character's occupation as a power-tools expert serving to emphasize the traditional gender roles of the characters.

At the same time, the late eighties and the nineties, more than any other era since, perhaps, the first years of television, has allowed for a diversity of family representations on television. In contrast to retro series like *The Cosby Show, Family Ties,* and *Home Improvement,* there is *The Simpsons* (which critic David Bianculli calls "the anti-Cosby"), *Married . . . with Children, Roseanne,* and *Grace under Fire,* all very popular series that have no illusions about the American family as a respository of sweetness and light. In the case of *Roseanne* and *Grace under Fire* (where Brett Butler plays a divorced mother who had been a victim of wife abuse), there is a level of realism and conviction that recalls the series of the 1970s. (A recent poll in *Parenting* magazine asked Americans which television programs most accurately reflected their lives. Forty percent picked *Roseanne,* 28 percent *Leave It to Beaver,* 7 percent *The Simpsons,* and 7 percent *The Addams Family.*)

The final noticeable trend in family series since the eighties is shows with unusual, sometimes outlandish, premises. If, for many years, television refused to recognize the changes in the American family, it now seems overeager to put families in the most unlikely circumstances imaginable. Consider:

• A Park Avenue bachelor adopts two black orphans from Harlem. (*Diff'rent Strokes*)
• Two bachelors raise an orphaned girl. Both had had affairs with the mother and don't know which of them is the father. (*My Two Dads*)

• The twenty-four-year-old oldest brother of five orphaned siblings moves back home to become his brothers' and sisters' legal guardian. (*Party of Five*)

• The oldest brother of seven orphans dresses up as their aunt so they will be allowed to live together as a family. (*On Our Own*)

• Two divorced mothers and their children form a new household together. (*Kate & Allie*)

• Two divorced fathers and their children form a household together. (*Dads*)

• Four divorced or widowed women form a household together. (*The Golden Girls*)

• A single father, a single mother, and their children form a household together, with the woman working and the man staying at home to keep house. (*Who's the Boss?*)

• A neurotic psychiatrist and his crotchety father form a household together. (*Frasier*)

• A widower enlists his brother-in-law and his best friend to help raise his three daughters. (*Full House*)

Undoubtedly, many of these variations are the result of sheer desperation for something new, with the widow-and-orphan device being a tried-and-true wild card for variation. At the same time, TV's decision to let a thousand families bloom (even if many of them don't correspond to a single real-life situation) must also to some degree be a tacit recognition of new and uncertain gender and parental roles, and of the fall from statistical (and perhaps cultural) preeminence of the "traditional" nuclear family.

Those changes, to bring this discussion full circle, can also be seen in the way American families *watch* TV: The early hopes of television as an agent of family unity have not been realized. In truth, it is one of the things keeping families (spatially) apart. Currently, more than a third of U.S. families own three or more television sets and receive (thanks to cable) an average of thirty-nine channels. Throw Nintendo and videocassettes into the mix, and the odds of the whole group sitting down together to watch a program are virtually nil. With the prominent exceptions of a few situation comedies, like *Full House* or *Home Improvement*, virtually every piece of programming is geared to a specific age and/or gender group, be it *Beavis and Butthead, Mighty Morphin Power Rangers, Monday Night Football, Masterpiece Theatre,* or *N.Y.P.D. Blue.* The *Wall Street Journal* recently described a Minnesota family of four with ten sets; the two daughters typically watch videos in the family room, the wife channel-surfs in the bedroom, while the husband watches sports downstairs.

So we have few illusions about television anymore. In a way, that is a heartening change. It now seems hard to believe that we once felt that a glowing box, programmed by Hollywood executives, would solve the family's problems. If anybody is going to do that, we now understand, it is going to have to be us.

CHAPTER IV

The Many Faces
of the American Family

Not long ago, Susan, a divorced single mother of an adolescent son, realized she wanted another child. She eventually adopted a Brazilian baby. The idea got her friend of many years, a woman named Cherry, to thinking. Cherry is a lesbian whose partners had never been interested in having a child, but she sorely wanted children in her life. She proposed to Susan that she would become a regular presence in the new baby's life, taking care of her at least one morning a week and being a member of her "family." It wouldn't be coparenting: Susan would pay the bills and make the major decisions. But it would be far more than baby-sitting.

And that's the way it has turned out. Cherry has become so attached to the baby, Abra, that she spends two days a week with her, not just one. She is present at all special occasions, is consulted about decisions affecting Abra's life, and is amply represented in the family photo album.

The story of Susan, Cherry, and Abra, told in journalist Anndee Hochman's fascinating book, *Everyday Acts & Small Subversions: Women Reinventing Family, Community and Home,* poses an interesting question: Are they a family? By any traditional or official definition, the answer is obviously no. But the world is changing very quickly, and so are the definitions. In end-of-the-century America, this is one of the ways a family looks.

In the previous chapters, you've heard the statistics, and learned a little bit about how they came to be. The time has come to give those statistics human faces, to give an idea of how it *feels* to be a family in America. I will do so in this chapter by giving a guided tour of the various aspects of the family today. When our expedition is over, we'll be ready for Part 2, a consideration of what can be, should be, and is being done to strengthen the family—and to help individual families—as we approach the year 2000.

FATHERHOOD:
YESTERDAY, TODAY, AND TOMORROW

The logical place to start would be with mother: mothers have traditionally been considered the veritable *center* of the family, setting the tone, establishing the standards, and taking responsibility for every other family member's diet, laundry, happiness, and emotional security. I know those days are over when I see all kinds of fathers wheeling baby strollers in the park or taking virtually equal responsibility for the care and nurturance of their children.

These "new fathers" are fighting a *very* long tradition of more or less distant, authoritarian fathers whose tempers always had to be feared (remember "Wait till your father gets home"?) and who, except for an occasional bedtime story or trip to the ballpark, left all child care and nurturing to mom. One of the clearest, most succinct expressions of this attitude came from the pen of the great Ernest Hemingway, who once warned new fathers, "When you have a kid, don't look at it for the first two years." Even sensitive Dr. Spock, in early editions of his *Baby and Child Care*, cautioned against "trying to force the participation of fathers who get gooseflesh at the very idea of helping to take care of a baby."

To be sure, we should be careful not to paint with too broad a brushstroke. Even in those dark days of the fifties and before, there were wonderful, nurturing fathers. My own, for example. One of my favorite early memories is of my father taking me to school. I would sit on the handlebars of his bicycle, in a special little seat he made for me, and we would practice multiplication tables. He would take me to synagogue every week and spend hours teaching me things—which was, I now realize, an unusual way to treat a girl in the rather sexist Orthodox Jewish culture. Later, when I was in the children's home in Switzerland during World War II, he wrote wonderful rhymed letters to me.

Still, the role of the father *has* changed dramatically over the last twenty-five years. When the movie *Mr. Mom* came out in the early eighties, it created an impression—and a catchphrase—because the notion of a man staying home to perform the traditional "house-wife" duties was such a novelty. Such a film would never be made today because real-life Mr. Moms are a dime a dozen. Among all fathers, there is a far greater amount of nurturing, involvement, and willingness to make career sacrifices for the sake of the family.

The most prominent examples, not surprisingly, are celebrities:

• A few years ago, the young daughter of NBC president Brandon Tartikoff suffered serious injuries in a car accident that necessitated treatment in New Orleans. Instead of letting his wife handle it alone, Tartikoff relocated from Los Angeles to Louisiana (hardly an entertainment-industry mecca) in order to be near his daughter.

• Movie director/producer George Lucas has sole custody of his three children, and he arranges his schedule so as to be with them as much as possible.

• Rock singer Billy Joel and tennis star Stefan Edberg both announced reductions in their schedules to be with and take care of their children.

• David Williams, a football player with the Houston Oilers, was fined $110,000 because he missed a game to be with his wife during childbirth.

• Saul Levmore, a professor at the University of Virginia, made headlines when he turned down an offer to be dean of the University of Chicago Law School because, he said, "I wanted to spend more time with my one-year-old son."

But it's not just a glitz-and-glamour thing. As a matter of fact, increased paternal participation in child-rearing is somewhat more noticeable among working-class families, where disproportionately more fathers have lost their jobs in recent years and have been *forced* to take care of home duties, than among upper-middle-class ones. In all, from 1988 to 1991, the percentage of fathers who were the primary caregivers for preschoolers shot up from 15 percent to 20 percent. (Significantly, the percentage of unmarried fathers who cared for their children rose from 1.5 percent to 7 percent.) These 2 million dads are served by several wonderful newsletters like *At Home Dad*, started by Peter Baylies, who has been at home with his son, John, since December 1992, when he was laid off from his job with Digital Equipment, the giant computer company. (You can reach Peter at 61 Brightwood Avenue, North Andover, MA 01845, or electronically at athomedad@aol.com)

I recommend the newsletter highly. It has recipes, tips of all kinds, personal essays, and in one recent issue I read a fascinating article about the stay-at-home dad to end all stay-at-home dads: Keith Dilley, father of sextuplets in Indianapolis.

Even in cases where the father isn't the primary caregiver, things have changed. A nationwide survey of fathers found that 81 percent reported taking a bigger part in child-care duties than their fathers did; 68 percent spend more time with their children; and 44 percent believe their children know them better as a person. And from 1977 to 1993, the percentage of married men who agreed with the statement "When making important family decisions, consideration of the children should come first" rose from 48 percent to 65 percent.

Unfortunately, this is not the whole story. Sociologist Frank Furstenberg coined the phrase "good dads–bad dads" to refer to the perplexing and somewhat troubling phenomenon of two simultaneous trends: one group of fathers who take their responsibilities ever more seriously, and another group who take them ever less seriously. The last trend is most visible among absent fathers (both divorced and never married) and it directly relates to the highly publicized phenomenon of "deadbeat dads." Of the 10 million women with children in fatherless homes, 67 percent get no child support at all. In all, of the $48 billion annually in court-ordered child-support payments, only $14 billion is paid. (The shortfall—$34 billion—is more than twice the cost of the federal Aid to Families with Dependent Children program, aka welfare.)

Then there are the absent fathers who don't even seem to be interested in having any contact with their children. More than one-fourth of absentee dads reported seeing their children less than once a month in the previous year, and one-fifth did not see them at all. For divorced fathers, this problem grows as time passes: The share of absentee fathers who never see their children born in a previous marriage increases from 2 percent within 2 years of separation to 31 percent by 11 years.

There is a grim result of this lack of contact. Generally, studies show that absence of the father (or some other male role model who's a regular part of their lives) can have direct adverse effects in boys, particularly if the separation from the father occurs before age five. In our culture, it is the fathers who have traditionally been expected to exert discipline and to provide an example for when aggression is appropriate or inappropriate; when they are absent, these issues are often unresolved. Studies indicate that fatherlessness is an indicator of delinquency, poor test scores, substance abuse, and other problems. Some 70 percent of long-term prisoners in U.S. penal institutions are men who grew up without fathers. And fatherlessness afflicts girls, too. A positive, loving, trusting relationship with a father is a model for how they will eventually relate to males in general. Girls who live in single-parent homes (which almost always means single-mother homes) experience 111 percent more teenage births, 164 percent more premarital births, and 92 percent more marital breakups than those from two-parent households.

Even in intact two-parent homes, the verdict is mixed. Despite all the talk about "new fathers," it is mothers who still perform the substantial majority of tasks related to child-rearing (as well as housework, cooking, etc.). A 1988 Harris poll found that 67 percent of men and 87 percent of women believed that husbands and wives should share family work equally, but that only 14 percent share equally in their own family. A recent survey of men with working wives and a child under five found that 30 percent of them did three or more hours of daily child care, compared with 74 percent of employed married mothers. Another study found that preschoolers worldwide spend an average of less than *one hour* alone with their fathers each day. (In the eleven countries included in the study, Chinese fathers spent the most time with their kids— fifty-four minutes a day. The worst country, interestingly, was Hong Kong, where the figure was six minutes. In the United States, it was forty-two minutes.) A 1990 survey of American businesses found that of the 1,000 companies that offered some form of paternity leave, only 1.3 percent of eligible fathers took advantage of the policy.

Lately there have been attempts, from a wide variety of quarters, to bring back absent fathers, and to emphasize the role of fathers in children's lives. The National Fatherhood Initiative is a well-funded and well-publicized organization dedicated to the cause. "It's been the wisdom of all human societies always that the father needs to be connected to the mother-child unit," says David Blankenhorn, the chairman of the organization and the author of *Fatherless America: Confronting Our Most Urgent Social Problem.* "The burden of proof is on our generation, which has struggled to do it another way, for the first time ever. All societies have struggled to get fathers involved, to keep them involved, through the institution of marriage. We are saying we don't think that's important."

There have recently been two large-scale summits on the question, both featuring the presence of Vice President Al Gore: Family Re-Union III: The Role of Men in Children's Lives, held in Memphis in July 1994, and the National Summit on Fatherhood, held in Dallas in October 1994. Out of Family Re-Union grew FatherNet, an Internet location where a wide variety of resources relating to fatherhood is available. For anyone with access to E-mail, FatherNet also conducts a listserv where people interested in fathering issues can communicate. (To subscribe, send an E-mail message to listserv@vml.spcs.umn.edu. On the first line of text type the following message: SUBSCRIBE FATHER-L <your E-mail address> <your first and last name>.)

It is absolutely essential that attention continue to be focused on fathers and fatherhood. But I will say in passing that some of the rhetoric and some of the attitudes of fatherhood proponents make me uneasy, especially when they bemoan the "androgynous" (which to my mind is just another word for egalitarian) marriage, or when they blame feminists (who supposedly claim fathers are unnecessary) for the problem. Wade Horn, the director of the National Fatherhood Initiative, has said, "What we are trying to counter is this sense in our culture that the mother and the father do the same thing. There is a sense that if the father is not changing 50 percent of the diapers, that if a father doesn't cry frequently in front of the children, then something is wrong with that father." And I would ask Mr. Horn, "All things being equal, why *shouldn't* fathers change 50 percent of the diapers?" The organization's literature also includes the following comments:

• "At times of crisis or stress, the traditionally male values—especially the ability to contain emotions and be decisive—are invaluable."
• "Father encourages risk-taking. Mother encourages caution."
• "When a child has difficulty at school, a family car is wrecked, or a dispute with a creditor arises, it is often the father who confronts the issue."

These are stereotypical images that have no basis in biology, just in cultural history. And when they are invoked, I feel that underneath it all is a secret wish to return to the old days, when the father had all the power. Naturally, not all fathers feel this way.

Vice President Al Gore, who is one of the keenest observers of American society I have ever had the pleasure of knowing, has publicly identified himself with fatherhood issues and made a major speech on the subject at the National Summit on Fatherhood in Dallas. His comments were incisive and they hit home. Consider the following excerpt:

He was nine years old when his mother first described the father who had deserted him when he was born. Eight years later, when he was a student at South Boston High, Marcellus Blanding wrote an essay about his reaction—and what he planned to do. He was going down South to see his father. He had some questions to ask him.

"What did you do after you got divorced? Was you thinking about my mother and me? Do you regret what you did to her? Do you still love her? What made you leave her? Do you want her back? What did you do all those years I didn't hear from you? Are you proud that I'm your son?"

And one more: "Wanna play me one on one in basketball?"

I am struck by the range of powerful emotion reflected in that short list. Marcellus Blanding is curious. He is resentful. He is wistful in the hope—so often echoed by the children of divorced parents—that his father might still love his mother. I read a hint of how deeply wounded he is when he asks of this father who doesn't know him: are you proud of me? And of course there is defiance—and a little anger. In the age-old tradition of sons who need to best their fathers, he is challenging his father to a little one-on-one.

These are the emotions we evoke when we think about one of the most complex, emotionally fraught relationships in the human experience: fatherhood. Too many American men have stepped away—consciously or unconsciously—from the most important role that any of us will ever play in life: that of protector, mentor and nurturer of the next generation.

There are those who point out how important fatherhood is strictly because of economics. Working men still earn four dollars for every three earned by women—and the children of divorce experience a 33% drop in income during the first year after a divorce. But for too long policymakers have defined the role of father as nothing more and nothing less than breadwinner. Focusing solely on economics ignores the stunting effect on fatherhood faced by the middle class dad who is working two jobs to make ends meet and can never be home for dinner. It ignores the damage done by the upper middle class dad who is so busy climbing the corporate ladder that he has no idea who his children's teachers are—or what they are learning in math, or who their friends are.

Defining the problem of fatherlessness as an underclass problem ignores the divorced middle class dads. Divorce sometimes puts a child in poverty but it *often* leaves the child without a father. Studies have shown that a large number of the children of divorce—20 percent in some studies—have not seen their natural father in five years. Even more haven't seen their father in a year.

Throughout this epidemic of fatherlessness, millions of brave single mothers have struggled to raise their children alone. Many have done wonderful jobs. But even the very best mother cannot replace the loneliness and sense of loss suffered by those children who have never known their father.

It is difficult in talking about this subject to ignore the facts of my own life. This is no academic matter for Tipper and me. We are lucky enough to be parents of four children.

Nothing quite prepares you for the experience: for moments like the time, ten minutes before the starting whistle of a soccer game, you have to turn to your children in the car and confess you're lost; or the ache you feel when you're thousands of miles away and each child gets on the phone for a few fleeting minutes of goodnight talk; or the first time you lose your temper and have to confess to yourself you've been totally wrong; or the times when a son or daughter who has been uncommunicative for days comes in chattering about the school play as if nothing is more valuable than to tell you what's going on.

Certainly nothing prepared me or Tipper for the knowledge of how brief a span we have before they are out of the house, to come home only on holidays, when looking up their old friends will seem a lot more important than hanging around the house.

This is the knowledge of maturity: the richness of the adventure of fatherhood set against the short time we have to experience it. It makes me want to urge all the fathers in this country—married, never married, divorced—to ask themselves the following questions: Do your children know where you came from? Have you given them a sense of your history and their history? Do your children know what you do every day? Have they ever gone to work with you? When was the last time you played a game with your children? When was the last time that you helped your children with their homework? When was the last time you went to your child's school and met with his or her teacher? And last, but certainly not least, do you treat your child's mother with respect? Even if you and she are still angry with each other, do you try hard to put your children first?

Not long ago, workmen were renovating the Baseball Hall of Fame in Cooperstown, New York. When they removed a display case, a snapshot fell to the floor. It was a picture of a man in a Sinclair Oil baseball uniform, holding a bat and smiling. There was no name.

But on the back was this note:

"You were never too tired to play catch. On your days off you helped to build the Little League Field. You always came to watch me play. You were a Hall of Fame dad. I wish I could share this moment with you. Your son, Pete."

The curators debated what they should do with this picture. They thought about putting it on display. They thought about launching a search to find out who the man was. But in the end they decided to put the picture right back where it had been, wedged under the display case, a secret memorial to every father who has taken the time to be there for his kids.

There may be no memorials for all who have worked so hard to restore meaning to fatherhood. But the future of our country rests in no small part on our ability to put our families back together. We may not know who the anonymous writer was. But we want the children of this generation to remember their fathers with the same unequivocal bond of affection.

DIVORCE, AMERICAN-STYLE

I've already sketched out the extent of divorce in America today and suggested some reasons as to why it has come to pass. What I want to consider now is how divorce has affected the lives of the mothers, fathers, and children involved.

The first thing I'll point out is that despite the popular image of divorce as an event that wrecks a home, in a growing number of instances there are no children involved. This could be because the divorce takes place before children are born; in fact, the *New York Times* recently discussed the trend of "starter marriages"—brief, childless unions of one or two years that, for whatever reason, seem to be becoming more common. Or it could be because the divorce takes place after children leave home. This trend makes sense for the generation that married young in the fifties and finds itself enjoying a longer life span than any group in the history of the world: That's more time to get *fed up* with each other. Whatever the explanation, the fact is that the average number of children involved per divorce reached a peak in 1964, at 1.34, and has generally been falling since then, to a current level of less than one. (In other words, most divorces occur in childless marriages.)

When children *are* involved in a divorce, it doesn't take a rocket scientist to see that, all other things being equal, the effects aren't great. No matter how often parents try to explain that the divorce has nothing to do with their feelings about the children, who will always be loved by both of them, how could kids not feel some combination of rejection and guilt when their parents tell them they're splitting up? ("If I had been a better girl and obeyed more often, Mommy and Daddy would still be together.") Matters get even worse in the frequent cases when the nonresident parent (usually the father) sees the child less and less frequently as time goes on. Let me quote Judith Wallerstein, an expert in the field, in the 1980 book she wrote with Joan B. Kelly, *Surviving the Breakup: How Children and Parents Cope with Divorce:*

> Children often feel abandoned or rejected by the parent who leaves the family home: younger children, especially, experience it as evidence of their own lack of worth. This blow to pride and self-esteem provokes anger in many children of divorce. . . . This sense of being rejected by the father, whether rooted in reality or primarily within the inner world of the young person, was linked significantly to poor psychological adjustment at the ten-year mark.

Compared to the population at large, adolescent children of divorced parents are less likely to graduate from high school, tend to marry at an earlier age, have a lower probability of ever marrying, and, if they do, are more likely eventually to be divorced themselves.

Joint custody, though difficult logistically and emotionally, seems to be the best way to mitigate against negative effects, instilling increased self-esteem and competence, and diminishing the sense of loss. Even frequent visits are beneficial. According to a recent article in the *American Journal of Orthopsychiatry*, "Many studies indicate that frequent contact by the absent father is a positive factor in development and that the frequency of post-divorce contact between father and daughter was found to be rather strongly correlated with the daughter's post-divorce perception of the father's love and that a low frequency of contact by the father contributes to a daughter's perception of him as rejecting and inconsistent in his life." In a laudable recognition of this state of affairs, California law expressly states that if sole physical custody is to be awarded, it should be to the parent who will provide the child with frequent and continuing access to the *other* parent.

But all studies of and statements about the negative effects of divorce have a central problem: It is *impossible* to tell what the effects on the child would have been if his or her parents had stuck out their unhappy marriage "for the sake of the children" because there is no control group. In other words, comparing children of divorce with the general population is statistically fallacious because the divorced group is self-selected: It consists of couples with problems so great that they eventually decided to divorce. If anybody can find a group of couples with problems of equal magnitude but who didn't divorce, *then* we will have some truly valuable studies.

There is no doubt that living in a home with continual stress and conflict, *regardless* of how many parents are present, is hardly beneficial for a child. One recent poll found that people whose parents had divorced were significantly more likely than people whose parents had "happy" marriages to agree with the statement, "When parents continually fight, children are better off if the parents divorce."

Another study looked at self-esteem of children in different family structures. When poverty was removed as a factor, there was no difference among the structures. The children with the lowest self-esteem came from intact two-parent families where the parents had a low level of interest. One possible explanation is that when there is a divorce, a child can explain (or rationalize) the noncustodial parent's lack of interest by blaming enmity between the parents. In two-parent homes, this explanation is not available.

"Divorce is not a good thing for children," says sociologist Frank Furstenberg, who, with Andrew J. Cherlin, wrote a classic book on the subject, *Divided Families: What Happens to Children When Parents Part.* "But it's not as consistent a negative effect as some people claim. Most people who have studied the subject believe it's better to grow up with one loving parent than two fighting parents."

But there is one incontrovertible negative effect of divorce: economics. One study found that women experienced a 73 percent drop in their standard of living after a divorce, while men experienced a 42 percent *improvement*. Throw into the mix the fact that women most often have custody of the child or children, the trend away from alimony payments, the fact that women consistently earn lower salaries than men even when performing the same jobs, and the well-documented failures of men to pay child-support, and you have a recipe for disaster. More than 25 percent of women (and their children, if there are any) fall into poverty at some point in the first five years after divorce. Divorced black women and their children are especially vulnerable: A 1988 study found that more than 61 percent of them were likely to be poor.

I know that, even had I not remarried, Miriam would not have been emotionally harmed by growing up without a father: She had enough love from me and my wonderful group of friends. But I wonder how high a standard of living I would have been able to provide for her, whether she would have been able to go to the best schools and live in a household where finances were not a constant concern, and I wonder what effect these uncertainties would have had on her.

But I did remarry, and in that I was not unusual. The United States has the highest remarriage rate in the world: Almost three-quarters of divorced men and about three-fifths of divorced women eventually acquire a new spouse, and the majority of children of single parents in time acquire a stepparent. The average length of time in a single-parent household is about six years, but it is likely to be much shorter for children whose parents divorce at an early age. In the United States today, 20 percent of households with married couples contain at least one stepchild under age eighteen, for a total of 5.6 million families.

In most cases, entering into a new marriage means a significant economic improvement for mother and children. It also has other benefits. Stepparents get a bad rap in fairy tales and other litera-ture, and no one would claim that the conflict-free, everything-rosy world of *The Brady Bunch* is in any way typical, but a stepparent is, if nothing else, another pair of hands. Anyone who's tried to raise children with only one pair knows how welcome reinforcements can be.

What is more, the prevalence of divorce has, ironically, created a kind of new extended family. Sociologist Ann Bernstein studied a family centered on the marriage of Carin and Josh, who have a mutual child. Josh was previously married to Peggy, with whom he had two children; they live with Peggy. Carin was previously married to Don, with whom she had two children, who live with her. Don then remarried Anna and had two more children, who live with them. All of these various steps and halves and exes see each other fairly regularly. And, in fact, a surprising number of these complicated clans manage to maintain ties from household to household. As sociologist Judith Stacey writes in her book *Brave New Families*, it is a case of "people turning divorce into a kinship resource rather than a rupture." In studying such extended families in the Silicon Valley of California, Stacey found that many people maintained a strong relationship not only with their ex-spouse, but with their ex-spouse's relatives: "Holidays and special occasions that might demand awkward or painful social decisions became instead affirmative rituals of expanded family solidarity." The moral is that in this day and age, we need all the family we can get.

But there are tensions and ambivalences in virtually all stepfamilies or "blended families" (as they are sometimes called in an attempt to remove the stigma). As anybody who has lived in such a situation can tell you, the possibilities of jealousy, resentment, discipline problems, or outright conflict are considerable, and can take years to resolve. (Studies have shown that the most pressure is on stepmothers, and that they have the hardest time.) Sociologists use the term "boundary ambiguity" to refer to uncertainty as to who is part of the family and who will perform which roles in it; it is certainly part of the territory in stepfamilies. You can see this in the issue of what to *call* the stepparent: Should she be "Helen," "Mom" or (heaven forbid) "Mrs. Smith"? A classic case of boundary ambiguity took place when Woody Allen left his lover, Mia Farrow, and began a relationship with her adopted daughter by a previous marriage. At least that was a consenting relationship. In a small but still alarmingly high number of cases, however, stepfathers sexually abuse their stepdaughters.

A recent survey pointed out the ambivalence by asking members of stepfamilies to name the members of their "family." Fifteen percent of those with stepchildren in the household didn't mention them. Among children, 31 percent didn't mention their stepparents and 41 percent didn't mention stepsiblings.

The society as a whole doesn't help matters. Despite the seeming ubiquity of such families in our culture, stepparents usually have to deal with an array of obstacles that are individually minor but collectively infuriating. Even though everybody individually knows better, our institutions seem to proceed on the assumption that everybody lives like Ozzie and Harriet. A doctor might refuse to discuss a child's medical condition with a stepparent, or a day-care center might not let a stepparent pick the child up, or an insurance package might not cover stepchildren. And despite stepparents' lack of rights regarding the stepchildren, they are not relieved of financial responsibility. For example, when a child's eligibility for college financial aid is considered, the stepparent's income is taken into consideration.

A major factor in determining the quality of stepfamily relationships is the age of the child or children at the time of remarriage: The older they are, the more the potential difficulties. If they are much past the toddler stage, it is only in rare cases that the stepparent will be viewed with the same degree of emotion and attachment as the biological parent. One family therapist suggests that the optimal role for a stepparent is somewhere between a parent and a trusted friend—what he calls an "intimate outsider."

I recently heard about a New Jersey woman—a stepchild, stepmother, and biological mother—who created and now markets a line of "Blended Families" greeting cards. One of them reads, "Combining our families takes love, patience and understanding. Let's work together!" And another: "Marriage made us 'in-laws' . . . But divorce doesn't make us 'out-laws.' Let's keep in touch!"

I am lucky; Fred adopted Miriam. I know this won't happen in all or even most cases, but I also know that almost all stepparents and stepchildren can achieve a warm, loving, and special relationship. In a word, they can be family.

GRANDPARENTS AND
OTHER FAMILY EXTENDERS

I was talking to a business associate the other day, and he told me of some interesting new developments in his family. His seventy-six-year-old mother-in-law, a widow, had just sold the New Jersey house where she had lived for fifty years and bought a condo in the Connecticut town where my friend lives with his wife and two small children. Why did she do it?

"To be closer to the grandchildren," my friend answered. "She takes a big interest in their education, and she realized that, being two states away, she just didn't see them enough."

And did he think she would miss her old life?

"Well, the fact is most of her friends have either died or moved away. Of the people who lived on the block when my wife was growing up, she's the last one left."

Now, this kind of arrangement is most definitely not for everyone. It presupposes a level of harmony between parents and children and daughters- and sons-in-law that is unfortunately rare. Many grandparents have jobs, friends, or other attachments that would keep them from making a change like that. And not everyone would be able to *afford* to make such a move.

But in cases where it could work, it struck me as a wonderful way of dealing with some of the family issues we face today. The grandparents get to be involved with the lives of their grandchildren. The (adult) children get some much-needed assistance in the raising of their little ones. And, in the process, the family is greatly strengthened.

In most human kinship systems over the course of history, grandparents have played an important role. They are the living link with the past, the repositories of wisdom. Sociologist Lillian Troll has referred to grandparents as "family watchdogs," always on the lookout for trouble and ready to provide assistance in the event of crisis. It has often been pointed out that some deeply emotional family bonds sometimes seem to skip a generation: There is so much mundane detail between parent and child—and frequently so much tension, so much obligation and unspoken expectations—that the relationship between child and grandparent takes on a special significance.

In her autobiography, *Blackberry Winter*, Margaret Mead describes her grandmother in terms that bring home to us how emotionally resonant a role it can be:

> She sat in the center of our household. Her room . . . was the place to which we immediately went when we came in from playing or home from school. . . . The strength of my conscience came from Grandma, who meant what she said. Perhaps nothing is more valuable for a child than living with an adult who is firm and loving—and Grandma was loving. I loved the feel of her soft skin, but she would never let me give her an extra kiss when I said good night.

In some cultures, most notably in the Far East, elders are still venerated, and the three- (or four-) generation home is common. In France, there used to be a law stating that when somebody built a house, there had to be an extra room for the *grand-mère*. In the United States, however, grandparents have been given short shrift for some time. A "definitive" book on the family published in 1955 did not include a single index entry for grandparents—not all that surprising, given the culture-wide emphasis on the nuclear family in the period. (We never saw—or even heard a mention of—Beaver Cleaver's grandfolks.) When grandparents were noticed, it was only in articles with titles like "The Grandparent Syndrome," which warned about the psychological problems that could result from their intrusive behavior.

But things have changed. Because of increased longevity and the ripple effect of the baby boom in baby boomers' children, there are more grandparents in America than ever before—currently more than 60 million of them, up 20 million over the past 15 years. Half of all people between 45 and 59 are grandparents, with 2 million of them having grandchildren living in the same house. And, because women stop bearing children at an earlier age, today's grandparents tend to be younger. In 1900, about half of all fifty-year-old women had children under eighteen; by 1980, the proportion had dropped to one-fourth. With the trend toward early retirement, grandfathers and grandmothers (if employed) have time to spend with their grandchildren, too. The average male can now expect to spend upwards of fifteen years in retirement from the labor force, compared to four in 1900.

What's more, with many baby boomers delaying having children, and then having only one or two, and a substantial minority not having children at all, today's grandparents average only three to four grandchildren, compared to twelve to fifteen in 1900, so they can lavish more time, attention, and money on each of them. *Toy Trade News* (which has an obvious interest in the matter) recently reported that the "grand ratio" (the number of grandchildren under 10 per grandparent) had dropped from 2.4 to 1 in 1950 to 1.2 to 1, and projected that it would fall to 1 to 1 by the year 2000.

The good part of all this is that each child, on average, gets *more* of his or her grandparents than previously. The bad part, as you know if you talk to a lot of people in their fifties and above, is that there's a serious grandchild shortage. I know many people who desperately want grandchildren, but find that their children won't cooperate.

These days, the terms of the relationship between the generations are likely to be different as well. Largely because of social security (but also due to trends toward wiser investing, more widespread pensions, and the general rise in the standard of living) grandparents are less likely to be economically dependent on their children, leaving them free to have a strictly emotional and loving relationship with them and their grandchildren. In fact, it is more common for grandparents to provide financial assistance to the younger generations, rather than the other way around. Many down payments for houses and tuition payments for college could *only* be made with the help of grandparents. As sociologists Andrew

Cherlin and Frank Furstenberg put it in their book *The New American Grandparent: A Place in the Family, A Life Apart*, "Bonds of obligation have declined relative to bonds of sentiment."

True, families are spread all over the country—with mom and dad in Florida, brother and his kids in Maryland, and sister and hers in Oregon—but technological advances have to some extent mitigated the effects of geographic fragmentation. As opposed to the old days, when you had to go over the river and through the woods in a horse-drawn sleigh to get to Grandmother's house, the telephone and the wide availability of air travel give us the illusion that she lives next door. I have no doubt but that in the years ahead the computer will make distant relatives seem even more accessible.

As a result of all these changes, instead of the stern, frail, somehow distant figure of years past, today's grandparent is younger, more accessible, more informal—something like a buddy or pal. In 1980 a sociologist polled college students and found that they expected grandparents to prefer the company of their peers and expressed the rather stereotypical view that grandparents "spoiled" their grandchildren. When asked the same questions in 1990, by contrast, students reported that it was very important for them to have a loving and warm relationship with their grandparents, that they were significant role models, that they shared family history with them, and that they had *fun* with them.

Grandparents who would like to arrange a trip with a grandchild should contact Grandtravel, a Maryland travel agency that will arrange intergenerational trips to the American Southwest, the Australian Outback, or pretty much anywhere in between. Grandtravel (which can be reached at 800-288-5575) prints a set of firm guidelines for behavior, such as being quiet in public places, no playing on elevators and escalators, and no littering.

The pressures of today's family life make the grandparent's role more vital than ever. When a child lives with only one parent or when his or her parents work long hours, a grandparent can seem like a knight in shining armor. Some live nearby, some move nearby, like my friend's mother-in-law, and some come to visit for extended periods of time. In the overwhelming majority of cases, they are far more than glorified baby-sitters. They can give their grandchildren a unique blend of love, the wisdom of the ages, and a sense of family heritage.

Of course, they don't really wear armor, and there are some real trouble spots to negotiate when it comes to determining the grandparent's role in the family. Along with the "pal" role has to come an acceptance that the grandparent in most cases will not be a figure of ultimate authority. Discipline will be a sensitive issue, as will disputes between husband and wife. Today's grandparents have to learn how to negotiate these rocky shoals—when to put their two cents in, and when to leave well enough alone. Studies show that beneficial influence of grandparents on children's development appears to be optimal when there is neither too little nor too much contact. But it's like the story of Goldilocks and the Three Bears. How much is just right? This is something every family has to work out for itself.

And while grandparents can seem like a godsend in the difficult period surrounding a divorce, there are problems as well. After divorce, it is often difficult for grandparents whose child (usually a son) does not have custody to maintain a relationship with the grandchild. Cherlin and Furstenberg write, "If your daughter's marriage breaks up, your relationship with your grandchildren will probably be maintained or even enhanced; but if your son's marriage breaks up, your relationship with your grandchildren is likely to be diminished in quantity and quite possibly in quality as well." Some grandparents have found that the custodial parent won't even let them see the children, leading most states to establish laws mandating grandparents' visitation rights.

Another troubling trend is the increasing number of grandparents raising grandchildren with neither parent present; currently, more than 1 million children are in this situation. There's nothing inherently wrong with this, but it is worth noting that the median income of grandparent-caregiver households is only $18,000, versus $36,204 for traditional households with children. And grandparent care usually is opted for as a matter of necessity, not choice—when the parents are deceased, substance abusers, incarcerated, child abusers, or just don't take responsibility for their children. In some inner-city communities, it is quite literally the grandparents (usually the grandmothers) who have kept family and community intact by housing and raising the children their own sons and daughters aren't prepared or willing to care for.

This is by no means a panacea. "In many states," notes Robin Warshaw, a journalist who has extensively investigated the "grandma crisis," "a grandmother raising grandchildren doesn't get foster care allotment—say, $800 a month—but only the Aid to Families with Dependent Children allotment—about $200 a month, plus $100 in food stamps. And although everybody is depending on them, these are not the ideal caregivers. Because so many of the grandmothers are poor and not in great health themselves and overworked, they are way old before their time. You see 50- or 55-year-old women who seem as if they're 80. Having to raise another set of children is an unfair burden for them. They often have had to give up a job that gives them satisfaction and a paycheck, and go on welfare instead. And once they're home with the grandchildren, they tend to be isolated."

In 1993, the *Washington Post* interviewed Daisy Carthens, a then seventy-seven-year-old grandmother of thirty-six, great-grandmother of fifty-eight, and great-great-grandmother of ten—three of whom lived with her. "I just do the best I can," said Mrs. Carthens. "I take them to church every Sunday, so no matter how things turn out at least I can say they knew right from wrong."

We can all applaud the dedication of such senior citizens, who roll up their sleeves and do the often grueling work of child care at an age when they should be sitting on the front porch and rocking. But it makes sense to ask, What will happen a decade from now and beyond, when (if current trends continue) these young children will *themselves* begin to have children? By that time, many of the current generation of grandparents will be too old to help out.

These are issues that will have to be faced in the years ahead. But there is no doubt that in the difficult world of the American family, grandparents are a key and irreplaceable resource, one that has increased in importance and will continue to do so as we approach the year 2000.

THE GAY NINETIES

I had not realized Hal was gay until he "came out" to me. We had worked together in the television industry for several years, and although TV is probably more accepting of diversity than most businesses, he still thought it prudent to keep his sexual orientation a secret except to close friends. Hal, fiftyish at the time, had been in a monogamous relationship with Paul, a pharmaceutical executive, for twenty years. As he said to me, "Neither one of us is exactly flamboyant."

Hal and Paul are still together, but in every other way their lives have dramatically changed since our conversation. Not long after that conversation they both took early retirement from their careers. They knew they wanted to leave Los Angeles, which they found faceless, and they spent a few years crisscrossing the country, trying to find the perfect place to live. They finally settled on a small Wisconsin town with a lot of old houses and artisans; they opened up an antiques store there, which is thriving. The other new development in their lives was . . . well, let Hal tell it in his own words:

> Paul has a cousin in Rochester that he's quite close to. Five years ago, Paul's cousin and his wife had their third child, and they asked Paul to be her godfather. The mother said, "I don't know anybody with stronger values." What's happened since then is that we've sort of adopted the other two children—they're nine- and thirteen-year-old boys—as well. We visit them at Christmas and at least one or two other times a year, and we've named them as the beneficiaries in our wills. We also spoil them blind. We've gotten them so much electronic

equipment—TVs, VCRs, computers—for their rooms that their mother said, "You may as well keep on buying that stuff. They already don't have any reason to leave their rooms."

Being a gay couple, we really don't have a lot of family left anymore. All four of our parents have passed away. And as we got older, we found that we missed not having family, children, and all the rest. At our age, we couldn't adopt. So you reach out, trying to find an extension to your own world.

It's interesting to watch the kids as they realize the nature of our relationship. The five-year-old just thinks we're friends. The nine-year-old is beginning to realize it. The thirteen-year-old is very much aware of it. He totally accepts it. When we walk into the house, he comes up and hugs us, with no sense of concern or discomfort with the fact that we're gay. If nothing else, we're showing at least one set of kids that gay people aren't all bad.

A continuing theme of this book is that, in view of all the tensions being experienced by the American family, it is imperative that we use the resources, the goodwill, and the love that are already out there. We will *never* bolster the family if we insist that it has to fit the old-fashioned, and in many cases outdated, model. And so our definition of family *has* to include prominent roles on the part of fathers, grandparents, stepfamilies, *and* gays and lesbians.

This includes not only cases like Hal and Paul's, wonderful as it is, but also gays and lesbians raising children, through adoption, artificial insemination, past heterosexual relationships, or other means. There are no good statistics available on how many of them there are; we have not yet reached the day when the Census Bureau includes such a question in its surveys, and many gays and lesbians are to some extent still in the closet. But I know a few, and I have friends and relatives who all know a few, so it's clearly a phenomenon. At this point, every U.S. state with the exception of New Hampshire and Florida has a law explicitly permitting gays to adopt, and many judges allow gays to adopt their partners' biological children. Not only do gay parents have their own support group—Gay and Lesbian Parents Coalition International, with sixty chapters—but their *children* have their own support group—Children of Lesbians and Gays Everywhere (COLAGE). And it's also clear to me that most of these families, unconventional though they are, have the kind of family values I believe in.

And so I get angry when I pick up the *New York Times* and read the headline, NEBRASKA MOVES TO BAR HOMOSEXUALS FROM BEING FOSTER PARENTS. The article goes on to say that the state—spurred by "conservative Christian groups"—is taking this action despite a chronic shortage of homes for foster children. And I get angry when I read about a Virginia judge's ruling that a divorced lesbian mother could retain custody of her child, but only if her partner did not live with them and her children never saw them in bed. ("It felt like my heart was being torn in half," the mother told a reporter. "I had to decide between my kids and my partner.") Or when I read about a Washington State gay man who had to deal with rumors that he was showing his three sons pornography. "I tore down all my curtains for a year," he told the *New York Times*, "so anybody could walk by and see what was happening in my house."

The case that's gotten the most headlines occurred in Virginia, where in 1993 Kay Bottoms petitioned to have her then two-year-old grandson taken away from his mother, Sharon Bottoms, simply because Sharon Bottoms is a lesbian. A court did so, giving custody to Kay Bottoms. Even though the Virginia Supreme Court overturned this decision in June 1994, the case has yet to be heard by the United States Supreme Court, and until it is, the boy remains separated from his mother.

This is absurd. The fact is that sentiments against gay parents are precisely that—sentiments. Some people don't *like* the idea of a little boy being raised by two "moms." But there has never been a scientific study showing any psychological ill effects on children raised by gay parents, nor (and this is the fear that lies under the surface) any effect on sexual orientation. No, what's important for a child is being raised by a parent—or, better yet, parents—who love and can provide for him or her. My feeling is that, because they really have to overcome obstacles in order to bear and/or raise children, and because the tragedy of AIDS has given them a heightened awareness of the need to affirm and continue life, gay people, in the majority of cases, make *exceptional* parents.

I know that's the case with a woman I know named Julie, a hospital administrator who raises two children with her partner Ellen, a lawyer. After they had been together nine years, Julie was artificially inseminated and gave birth to Katie, who's now seven; three years later, Ellen gave birth to Max. Interestingly, the same (anonymous) donor supplied the sperm for both kids, so, biologically, they're half-siblings.

They live in a big old house in an area of Philadelphia with "dozens" of women in similar circumstances, so they don't feel isolated at all. Of course, it helps if you have a sense of humor. "When Katie was about ten days old, we were out shopping and Ellen had her in a Snugli," Julie says. "A woman asked how old the baby was, and when Ellen told her, she said, 'You look *wonderful.*' Of course, I was completely bedraggled, but I didn't say anything."

The kids call both mothers Mom, switching to Julie or Ellen if further clarification is needed. So far, Max has no clue that there's anything unusual about his circumstances. "Once every few months," Julie says, "Katie will say, 'I wish I had a dad. I'd still have two moms, but it would be like Sharon, Lois and Bram [the kids' singing group].' I just say, 'Oh, well . . .' Actually, she's very melodramatic, and about once every *week* she makes a big production about wanting to move back to the house we moved out of a year or so ago, so I don't see the dad business as that big a concern."

Julie and Ellen realize the importance of male role models, especially for Max. "Ellen's parents moved from New York to Philadelphia when Katie was one and a half," Julie says, "and their grandfather is very important in both kids' lives. They have godfathers, and Ellen's brother and my brother are uncles who are very important to them.

"When I hear people say a child needs a father, I take that to mean that, if possible, it's better to have two *parents*. And I absolutely agree."

Lately, Julie says, Katie has developed an interest in boys. "She's a real vamp. She pulls her shirt down over her shoulder and giggles a lot about boys. I don't know where she gets that from," Julie says with a laugh. "Probably the donor."

Phyllis Burke, author of *Family Values*, a book about raising a son with her lover, encountered remarkable hostility when she went on a nationwide tour to promote the book. "Sometimes it was amusing," she told the *San Francisco Chronicle*. "One host began by saying, 'Would you give your sperm to a lesbian?' Other times it was arduous. People asked, 'Who's going to teach him to be a man?' and 'How will he know the difference between a man and a woman?' Men on car phones seemed to be the most angry."

But it was a man on a car phone—a white fundamentalist in Toledo, to be exact—who gave her the most heartening response of all. "I've decided," he said, "that it's very important for any child to have one parent who loves them unconditionally the way this lady is talking about. But to have two parents who love them unconditionally the way this lady is talking about, to have two parents who love you that way, any kid has to be lucky."

THE BLACK FAMILY

In 1964, Daniel Patrick Moynihan, then a domestic policy aide to President Lyndon B. Johnson, was asked to look into the situation of the black family. His report, published in 1965 as *The Negro Family: The Case for National Action*, has set the terms for all subsequent discussion. He blamed the failure of African Americans to make adequate economic and social gains on the African American family—specifically, its tendency to take the form of a matricentric, rather than a two-parent, home. The black family, Moynihan concluded, was "a tangle of pathology." "The evidence," he wrote, "is that the Negro family in the urban ghettoes is crumbling."

Many books and scholarly articles have been written in response to the Moynihan report; this is not the place, and I am not the person, to go over all that ground yet again. But I will say a few things. First of all, Moynihan (who is now my senator) was absolutely correct in observing the trend toward mother-centered households in the black community. And, as I noted earlier in the book, the trend has dramatically accelerated in the thirty years since then. As of 1993, in 58 percent of all black family households with children, only the mother is present, compared to 37 percent where both parents are present and 5 percent where only the father is present. (Among whites, the figures are 20 percent with only the mother present, 76 percent with two parents present, and 4 percent with only the father present.)

Moynihan was correct, too, in saying that, all things being equal, it would probably be better for black people—just as it's better for *all* people—to grow up in two-parent homes. That way, there is more of everything to go around: money, role-modeling, attention, time, and love.

But he was wrong, too. First of all, he erred in his implication that the black family had *always* been matricentric, possibly in keeping with its African heritage. A host of scholars since then, most notably Herbert Gutman, author of *The Black Family in Slavery and Freedom*, have demonstrated that even in the days of slavery, and certainly in the years following the Civil War, the black family was characterized most prominently by the two-parent model. Through painstaking historical research, Gutman demonstrated that between 1855 and 1880, between 70 and 90 percent of black families had a husband or father present and two or more members of a nuclear family unit.

Indeed, if anything, black Americans have traditionally placed more, not less, of an emphasis on family values and family ties than white Americans have. Consider the incredible sacrifices necessary to keep families together in the slavery era—when masters often deliberately split up husbands, wives, and children—and in the Jim

Crow days of severe discrimination and oppression that followed. Nevertheless, between 1900 and 1950, black men were statistically just as likely to marry as white men were, and black women were *more* likely to marry than white women.

But that changed, slowly at first and now more rapidly. Moynihan put the responsibility for this—the blame, really—on blacks themselves. So do many contemporary observers. To take one example out of hundreds, Virginia Senator Charles Robb has said that in his father-in-law Lyndon Johnson's time, "racism, the traditional enemy without," was the problem; today, "it's time to shift the primary focus . . . to self-defeating patterns of behavior, the new enemy within." One hears this kind of rhetoric time and time again, from blacks as well as whites, from conservatives (anyone from Dinesh D'Souza to Newt Gingrich), from moderates (like Bill Clinton), and from liberals (like Jesse Jackson).

And on an *individual* level, it is absolutely correct. It is a matter of self-interest—and of societal interest—for a person to strive to be as productive, moral, and family centered a citizen as he or she possibly can. But on a global level, this is a classic case of blaming the victim. The reason the black family has tended toward the single-mother model in the years since the end of World War II is not any moral failing, irresponsibility, or lack of backbone on the part of blacks, or because of the attractiveness of welfare payments, but because black men, historically the victims of racism, now have had to face a steady drying up of economic opportunity.

Starting in about 1940, blacks in great numbers began moving from the South to the North in the "great migration." They came because of the promise of jobs, and there were periods when it seemed as though this promise would be kept—like the boom of the late forties, when factories were expanding and hiring, and the Great Society period of the midsixties, when it seemed that the country was committed to its cities. But for the most part, steady, well-paying industrial jobs have gradually but relentlessly disappeared over the decades, lost to rural America, to foreign countries where labor is cheap, or merely in the "deindustrializing" transition to the low-wage "service economy." Even when blacks were hired for such jobs, on the "last hired, first fired" principle, they were the first to be let go when the next recession or slow period hit.

And so, in the recessionary period between 1979 and 1984, half the black workers in durable-goods manufacturing in the Great Lakes region lost their jobs. The city of Detroit is perhaps the most striking example of these trends. It has lost half its jobs to deindustrialization and half its population, both to "white flight" and, what is equally important, to the suburban migration of those blacks who have managed to make their way to the middle class. What's left behind is a devastated city.

University of Chicago sociologist William Julius Wilson, in his book *The Truly Disadvantaged*, documented just how disastrous an effect these economic circumstances have had on the institution of marriage. He found that men with jobs were over two and a half times more likely to marry the mother of their child than were unemployed men. And he found that for every 100 black women aged 20 to 24 in Chicago in 1980, there were only 45 employed black men of the same age.

Those unemployed men don't marry their children's mothers, says University of Pennsylvania sociologist Elijah Anderson, author of *Streetwise: Race, Class, and Change in an Urban Community*, because "they don't have a stake in the system. They don't have much to lose. If they did have some economic hope, if they did have something to lose by getting a girl pregnant at the age of 16, then they wouldn't do it. If they had a stake, you would see many more of them forming families and mimicking other kinds of middle-class behavior."

The other thing that Moynihan and his ideological kin overlook are the *strengths* of the black family. First of all, all the rhetoric about "pathology" and "crumbling" has obscured the presence of millions of black families of the "traditional" variety—mother, father, and children—many of whom have established and maintained their households in the face of extremely difficult circumstances. As for the single-mother family unit, it is surely not the optimal vehicle for blacks to advance economically or socially, especially among the lowest-income groups, who are least equipped to go it alone. Nevertheless, in many ways the black family has been an adaptive, brave, and in some ways exemplary response to the conditions faced by black people in this country.

"A lot of people took umbrage at the Moynihan report," says Elijah Anderson, "especially since the history of the black family had been so noble. Look at the effort people went through to keep families together during slavery and its aftermath. That so many families did remain intact is a remarkable accomplishment.

"It was due largely to the efforts of women. They were not beaten down in the same way as men were, first by their masters, then by white men as a group. Black women were not regarded as the same order of threat, so they were the ones who carried families and society, the ones who provided for and socialized the next generation."

The greatest strength of black families—and a quality likely to be overlooked by today's whites, given their fixation on the fifties-style nuclear family—is their awareness of, identification with, and loyalty to the *extended* family. In nineteenth- and twentieth-century urban America, Stephanie Coontz writes in *The Way We Never Were*, "African-American families maintained tighter and more supportive kin ties than did other urban families, taking care of elders, paupers, and orphans within family networks rather than institutionalizing them as frequently as other groups did."

The black family has built up a toughness over the years, and ties tend to remain unbroken even in difficult circumstances. And so even the single-parent family statistics, suggesting that children are growing up in isolation, are deceiving. One national study, for example, found that poor African American absent fathers had more contact with their children and gave them more informal support than middle-class white absent fathers.

You can see this resilience, too, in the legion of grandmothers who take in their daughters' (and sometimes sons') children. This is a part of the broader practice of "informal adoption," quite common in the black community, where kids are taken in and cared for—temporarily or permanently—by relatives or friends. A *New York Times* article described Mary Connolly, a fifty-year-old New

York psychotherapist who raised a nephew from age six to sixteen, took in his eleven-year-old sister when she came to New York from North Carolina to run in track tournaments (and kept her until she turned twenty), and in 1993, when the article was written, was raising the nephew's five-year-old daughter, who called her Mommy.

This broad, inclusive, and expandable conception of "family" definition is one tradition that *does* seem to have roots in Africa. Historian John Henrik Clarke, himself informally adopted at age fourteen when his mother died, was struck when he visited Ghana not long ago and met a man who introduced him to his seven mothers. "He said, 'This is my mother, this is my senior mother,' and he called everybody in his mother's age group his mother," Clarke told the *Times*.

The strengths of the black family are most strikingly evident in the massive family reunions that have become extremely popular in the black community since the publication of Alex Haley's *Roots* in 1976. Dozens, hundreds, or sometimes more than a thousand members of extended clans will meet every year for a long weekend of celebration, workshops in drug prevention or family-tree construction or running for political office, fashion shows, some just plain catching up, and—last but not least—for some really serious eating.

Ione Vargus, a presidential fellow at Temple University and the chair of Temple's Family Reunion Institute, had been attending her own family's annual reunions since 1980, and her enjoyment of the events led her to publish a scholarly study of reunions in 1986. That in turn led to the establishment of the Family Reunion Institute, which each year holds a conference on the subject, attended by about 200 people.

"When I started going to different reunions and observing them, I began to see their tremendous potential," Vargus says. "Families weren't doing them for any sociological reason—they were doing them because they love family. But so many positive things would emerge. There were people trying to trace their roots, doing genealogical research, telling stories of ancestors. That instills a sense of identity, self-worth, self-esteem. I love the workshop idea, because it lets people get to know each other, and it allows you to bring up issues without pointing fingers. You can have a workshop on teen pregnancy led by young people.

"There's also quite a bit of self-help, such as scholarship funds. There's typically a wide range of people who attend, from affluent families to people on welfare. So there are all kinds of role models—here's someone who's a good father, here's someone who's been educated, here's someone who's achieved.

"The reason all this can get accomplished is that the reunions are so much fun. Often when a couple is divorced, the spouse who's not part of the family will still attend the reunion—they don't want to give that up. On several occasions, I've seen a woman family member there—and her ex-husband is there with his new wife!"

The point that's important to remember is that statistics aren't people, particularly when you talk to someone like Beverly, a thirty-seven-year-old black woman who lives outside Philadelphia. She was born in a tiny town in Virginia, but moved to Philadelphia as a toddler when her father, a farmworker, decided there would be better opportunities in the North. He found work as a longshoreman, and before long bought a house in a solid working-class part of West Philadelphia.

It seemed that Beverly's family fit the basic American middle-class model. But it didn't. "My parents were alcoholics," Beverly says. "Their drinking went on all throughout my childhood, but I didn't realize it until I was a teenager. Then I wanted to get out." Beverly got involved with the Jehovah's Witnesses, and through the church met the man she would marry. She was eighteen years old.

"I thought marriage was my only ticket away from my home life, but I was too young. He was only twenty-one; neither of us realized the responsibilities involved."

After six months, she comprehended her mistake, but the Jehovah's Witnesses don't permit divorce except on the grounds of adultery, and that was one of the few difficulties the couple *didn't* have.

Soon they had a son, Christopher, but that didn't solve their problems—it never does—and eventually they were separated.

Beverly wasn't completely on her own. Her husband gave her child support, and his mother, with whom she had a good relationship, let her live in an apartment, rent free. She did temporary office work, went to school for a while to study fashion design, then hit on a job that suited her even better.

"I met someone through the church who had a cleaning business," she says. "I had always looked down on cleaning. I'd always said I'd never go into white people's houses, the way my mother had. But this person explained to me that you didn't *have* to do it that way—have them pick you up at the bus stop, make lunch for you. You could run it as a business. I decided I would carry and conduct myself a certain way—so it was clear I wasn't going to be someone's 'cleaning lady.' And I charged enough so that I could do the work and feel good about myself. Now, my rate is up to twenty dollars an hour. If people don't want to pay it, that's fine. But if they do, they know they're getting into a professional relationship. The other good thing was that on most jobs, I could take Christopher with me."

Eventually, she got the grounds she needed for divorce. The cleaning business was going well, and she thought she would never marry again, but then, through the church, she met Steve, a soft-spoken musician who was working as a security guard to make ends meet. They had a lot in common—he was divorced with three children—they became friends, and they fell in love.

"When I first started going out with Steve, Christopher said, 'Momma, are you going to marry Steve?' I said, 'Well, when you feel we know him well enough, you let me know.' Soon after that, he started calling him Daddy. That's been their relationship right from the beginning."

After they were married, Steve and Beverly operated the cleaning business together for a while. Then he took a job as a bus driver with a wealthy suburban school district—for the security and benefits; on weekends and some evenings, he plays music for senior citizens in nursing homes. After a few years, they put all their financial resources together, took a deep breath, and moved from the city to the suburbs, which is known for its excellent school system and is predominantly white.

"I had always lived around black people," Beverly says. "I found it hard to be in this environment at first and wanted to move back to the city. But not only did Steve say no—Christopher did, too," she says with a laugh.

The business is thriving, Christopher is doing well in school, and Beverly has found, almost to her amazement, that a family life far different from the one she grew up in is attainable. "I have a lot of wealthy friends," she says, "and they all say to me, 'You and Steve—you're living the American dream.' "

PUT THEM ALL TOGETHER
AND THEY SPELL . . .

It's Tuesday, so by 2:50 in the afternoon the mad rush will be on. Sue, a physical therapist in a suburb of Chicago, will tear out of the office, race to the car, and attempt to get to four-year-old Sam's preschool by the three-o'clock closing, then come home, where middle-schooler Bill will have let himself in. Six-year-old Katie and nine-year-old James walk in from their bus stop at three-thirty.

"Then," Sue says, "we have activities."

Young Sam has gymnastics class at four, before which a piano teacher has arrived at the house to give James a lesson and a local college student has come to "enrich" Bill in history. Sue will drive to the gym at five to pick Sam up and drop Katie off for *her* lesson, then it's back to home to start making supper, and back to the gym to pick up Katie at six. And tonight, Katie has a birthday party at six-thirty.

"Afternoons are very hectic," says Sue, in what might be the understatement of the decade.

Sue has worked part time since Bill's birth, and now works just two days a week in a distinctive job-sharing arrangement. She and the other woman, also a mother, work nine to three (in Sue's case, 2:50) and, by doing all their paperwork during their lunch hour, manage to complete a forty-hour job in just thirty hours. (Even so, Sue often has to take work home.)

Undoubtedly, the hectic quotient could be dramatically reduced if Sue gave up her job. After all, as her husband, Joe, often says, "You run a business here." And while her salary is nice, it's not truly essential to their budget, since Joe is a surgeon and makes an excellent living.

But she *won't* give up her job. "Family is my thing, but work is also my thing," she says, in the Texas drawl she still hasn't lost after all these years. "It's part of my identity, and that's why I won't give it up. It's the one thing I can call my own. And in an odd way, it's relaxing. I can concentrate on helping one patient at a time, which is a lot different from dealing with four kids simultaneously."

Come to think of it, "hectic" might be a good one-word description of motherhood as we approach the year 2000. It is a time when the old images and ideals are rapidly changing, yet the new ones haven't been fully established to take their place. The result is a mixture of confusion, anxiety, excitement, guilt—and a lot of rushing around.

That old image was a rather peculiar one. From the Victorian era on, society has had a somewhat sentimental view of mom, imbuing her with emotion as the keeper of the family flame. Yet, at the same time, we have also asked her to do the grunt work of the household, with no pay and precious little respect. Stranger still, the assumption behind this view—that the mother's role as caregiver and nurturer is somehow biologically determined—has little or no basis in fact.

"The image of the stay-at-home mother who devotes herself to the children is a historical aberration," says Dr. Shari Thurer, a Boston University psychologist and the author of *The Myths of Motherhood: How Society Reinvents the Good Mother*. "It never happened before because birth control wasn't available. Women would have a *series* of children. That, and the fact that they were over-whelmed with domestic tasks, meant that they could never devote a large quantity of time to any one child.

"Biologically, there is no such thing as a maternal instinct. As part of the human species, both men and women are going to want to protect and preserve their children. Sure, only women can give birth to and feed babies—but there's no way to show they have an inherently stronger attachment or are somehow meant to be in charge of child care. The fact is, dads were kicked out of the home after the industrial revolution created a division of labor by gender. Because of that, they have had less contact with kids over the last century or so. But, given the right circumstances, dads can be won-derful mothers."

Today's mothers have what W. E. B. Dubois, in writing about black Americans, referred to as a "dual consciousness." They realize that the notion of mothers having some special powers, capacities, and abilities when it comes to children and home is a culturally de-termined myth. Yet at the same time, being products of that cul-ture, they to some extent cannot help believing and participating in the myth. *New York Times* columnist Anna Quindlen once beauti-fully expressed some of the resulting ambivalences:

How well I remember, some years ago, the frisson of fear when I read that part of the evidence against Mary Beth Whitehead, in her battle to keep the child she'd conceived in a surrogate arrangement, was the testimony of a psychiatrist that she had played pattycake incorrectly. The mother of two young children at the time, I wondered: am I playing right?

There is a clear double standard for mothers and caregivers. One mother at the park laced into a departing sitter, com-plaining that she'd spent all her time talking to her friends while the children played nearby, oblivious to the fact that she and I were doing the same. Another once told me that she could not imagine how a family day-care provider could ade-quately care for three small children at once, either unaware that I had three such myself or confident that mothers had magical powers. . . .

So let's not perpetuate this cult of the perfect pattycake mother, who renders all other options suspect and second-rate. It pits women whose children are cared for in part by others and worry that they rob them of this ideal childhood against women who care for their kids full time and wonder why they cannot measure up to the ideal. It assumes a uniformity to our families, our kids and our own abilities that is simply illusory. And it sets us all up for failure.

As noted earlier, women—specifically, mothers—have entered the workforce en masse over the last quarter-century. In many ways, this social movement has had an extremely beneficial effect on the American family. In American culture, to put it simply, money talks, and the fact that more women now contribute to the family finances has made them more equal partners in the family dynamics. Most women who work find that having a job or career makes them feel better about themselves; children pick up on this self-esteem, and unquestionably benefit from it. Equally beneficial is the demonstration of egalitarianism between husband and wife, mother and father; it provides a powerful positive example for the children.

Consider, in this regard, the difference in the American TV family from Ozzie and Harriet to Roseanne. The house is messier, and so are the interactions. Both parents work, so they don't spend the same *quantity* of time with the kids. But are the kids any worse off? Are they loved any less? Author Barbara Ehrenreich thinks not. "She's genuinely interested in those kids," Ehrenreich writes of Roseanne Conner. "She finds ways to get them to talk about the hard things without invading their space." I agree.

At the same time, the mass entry of mothers into the workplace has been responsible for much of the pressure that the middle-class American family now feels. A couple of generations ago, it was assumed that mom would man the home front. With mom at the office, the home front is clearly understaffed.

To be sure, society has adapted to some extent. Some (but not enough) companies have introduced such family-friendly policies as extended maternity and paternity leave, flex time, and on-site child care. Some (but not enough) fathers are stepping up their contributions to the household. Relatives have pitched in, and, most of all, mothers themselves—like Sue—have been enormously creative, adaptive, energetic, and resourceful in finding ways to combine the twin demands of family and work.

Working Mother magazine and the Gallup organization recently polled 1,000 working mothers and came up with some heartening findings. Here is how they responded when asked if they were "very" or "extremely" satisfied in various areas:

How well your children are doing: 84 percent
The job you're doing as a mother: 82 percent
Your work: 69 percent
Your marriage: 67 percent
Managing the demands of work and family: 54 percent

But everything is not hunky-dory, as the dropoff toward the end of the above statistics indicates. While women don't stint on the children, and by and large are delighted with how they are doing, you really *can't* have—or do—it all. The fact is, as most working mothers will tell you, working mothers have extended themselves beyond the call of duty, and the rest of society simply hasn't followed suit. This can be seen most egregiously in the insufficient availability of high-quality day care. A 1994 national survey of day-care centers found that just 12 percent were "good" or "excellent," 74 percent were adequate, and 12 percent were less than minimal. For infant and toddler care, 40 percent were rated less than minimal, meaning that hygiene was poor, there were safety problems, babies weren't held enough, and there weren't appropriate toys. This isn't a family problem, it is a *national* problem, and until we solve it, we as a country will not be able to "manage the demands of family and work."

Needless to say, it is mothers who have had to bear the brunt of the responsibility for this problem. Many have devised ingenious job-sharing arrangements (like Sue) or part-time schedules, by telecommuting from home, or by starting their own businesses that will allow them to allot their time as they see fit. A growing number have been able to do so by stopping work altogether. A Virginia organization called Mothers at Home, which was created "to help mothers at home realize they have made a great choice" and "to help mothers excel at a job for which no one feels fully prepared," has more than 15,000 members nationwide.

I applaud these women for taking what in many social circles amounts to a courageous step; *not* working is sometimes stupidly seen as an indication that a woman is less intelligent than someone who does. But at the same time, in no way do I denigrate those who are still in the workplace, women who are forced to suffer their own pangs of guilt about not living up to the ideal. The goal, of course, would be *no* needless guilt, and a society where the responsible personal choices of men and women both were honored, respected, and supported. Not long ago I clipped a letter to the *New York Times* from a Maryland woman that made this point very well:

> Two groups of mothers are on the defensive today: full-time mothers who worry about their lapsed careers and full-time employees who worry about their children. Discourse between them has become virtually impossible. Mothers in each group have a troubling tendency to justify their child care decisions by making sweeping attacks on the other group. . . .
>
> Years ago a study found that the best predictor of success for children was happy parents: whether their mothers worked or stayed home proved immaterial. . . .
>
> I hope that women will someday have enough self-confidence to justify their own decisions without denigrating the choices that are made by others, and to read the conclusions of noted child care experts with more detachment.

PART 2

And What to Do about It

CHAPTER V

Whose Family Values?

Saying that the American family has some serious problems is not exactly a reason to stop the presses. For one thing, if that fact hasn't been made clear to you by the time you've gotten this far in the book, then you haven't been paying attention. For another—and more significantly—over the last five years or so there has been a general consensus in our society that the quality of family life in this country has precipitously declined. The expression of the consensus can be seen in talk shows, cover stories, editorials, political speeches, and, yes, books—at this point, the assumption of family crisis is so prevalent that a case for it doesn't even have to be made.

I said that the consensus has been in effect for five years or so, but I can date the moment when it crystallized more exactly than that. It happened in the summer of 1992, when Dan Quayle, running for a second term as vice president, made the famous address that would forever after be known as the Murphy Brown Speech. Interestingly, the reference to the television character played by Candice Bergen took up only a small fraction of the speech (given to the Commercial Club of San Francisco). The speech, you may recall, was given shortly after days of widespread looting, destruction, and general chaos in south-central Los Angeles, and, in essence, was an attempt to explain the riots as a result of a breakdown in family values.

Looked at point by point, much of what Quayle said was hardly controversial. "It's time to talk again," he stated, "about family, hard work, integrity, and personal responsibility." Who could argue with that?

"We cannot be embarrassed," he added, "out of our belief that two parents, married to each other, are better in most cases for children than one." And who would possibly *attempt* to embarrass anyone out of this belief—especially with that key phrase, "in most cases," strategically placed in the sentence?

No, few would argue with these statements (though Quayle and some of his allies like to transform their political opponents into straw men—and women—with nothing but contempt for family, hard work, and so forth). The problem with Quayle's speech is where he went from this starting point. First of all, he claimed that the L.A. riots were a result of people not hewing to the values he was extolling. This reasoning is supportable, though debatable, but it ignores a much more cogent explanation for the antisocial behavior. Over the previous eleven years, the economic standing of poor people—especially poor black people—in this country had gotten much worse, with real income decreasing, opportunities drying up as a result of deindustrialization and job loss, and government support declining in real terms. Of course, it was understandable that Quayle might not have wanted to mention this state of affairs, because the people running the country during those eleven years were his boss, George Bush, and Bush's predecessor as president, Ronald Reagan.

Even more troubling was Quayle's interpretation of the cause of the family-values breakdown. There were two villains, as he saw it. One was "the turbulent legacy of the sixties and seventies," with its disdain for tradition, its me-first selfishness and hedonism, and its reflexive iconoclasm. (I think it will be the *twenty*-sixties before politicians will stop using the 1960s as a scapegoat for every social ill they can think of.) The other was Hollywood, whose films and television programs, as Quayle saw it, promoted irresponsible behavior and heaped scorn and abuse on anyone who thought and acted otherwise.

Enter Murphy Brown. The character on the popular CBS comedy series—an anchorwoman for a *60 Minutes*-type TV magazine show—had just decided to have a baby out of wedlock, without benefit of a husband or even a father who was expected to hang around after impregnating Murphy. No, all that was wanted from him was his sperm. According to Quayle, putting forth this scenario as a model of behavior was reprehensible, not only in itself but because of all the people who would consciously or unconsciously imitate it.

Now, I have no problem with the idea of taking the behavior and characters depicted in books, plays, or TV shows seriously, or with passing judgment on them in the contexts of our own lives. Very wise people have done so for years—starting with the Bible and moving all the way up to Forrest Gump. I myself have long criticized the media for the frequently cavalier way it portrays sexual behavior—particularly the way people are forever being shown having sex without benefit of condoms or other birth control, but are almost never shown as suffering any negative consequences from this omission. I am equally convinced that the near-ubiquitous violence in films and television is a bad thing—not only in and of itself but in the possibility that impressionable young people will conclude that this is an acceptable, even a desirable, way to behave.

Moreover, I even had my own misgivings about what we were shown in the series concerning Murphy Brown and her baby. Certainly, if a woman (or a man) finds for whatever reason that marriage is not in the cards, then she (or he) is entitled to consider the option of having a child on her or his own. And a single woman (or man), especially one with the moral fiber, the sense of humor, the intelligence, the good friends, and (last but *not* least) the income that her scriptwriters have given Murphy Brown, has the ability to raise a wonderful kid without a partner. I started to do so myself, with all those attributes, I can modestly say, except the last. And although I am supremely happy that I met and married Fred Westheimer, I have no doubt that Miriam would have turned out just fine even if he had never entered the picture. Indeed, the very fact that Murphy Brown made the conscious *decision* to have a child gives her a leg up on many, many other mothers (myself included), for whom pregnancy is "accidental" and who are very likely not prepared or even eager for what is to come.

On the other hand, I'm not sure the producers and writers of the program took seriously enough what they were getting Murphy into. Maybe they could have devoted a little time to exploring why marriage *wasn't* in the cards for her, so as not to give the impression that they had disdain for the entire institution. And maybe they could in some way have shown her internal deliberations, so essential in making a decision like that, and something that doesn't always fit smoothly into comedy.

Nevertheless, to suggest, as Quayle did, that this television show had a significant effect on the behavior of Americans is ludicrous. I know a great many women, and I don't know a single one who really thinks of her life as in any way like that of Murphy Brown, or who would take any action based on the fact that Murphy Brown did the same thing. Murphy Brown is a fantasy, and I would credit the American people with understanding that.

But the truly and deeply disingenuous thing about Quayle's speech was the link to the L.A. riots. The idea that Murphy Brown's single motherhood had anything to do with young, single black girls getting pregnant and having children—or with those children growing up to take part in antisocial behavior—makes about as much sense as blaming me for the bad enunciation of Americans. No, I think what Quayle really wanted to do was to blame the plight of the poor people of Los Angeles on their own moral laxity and "selfish" behavior, their lack of family values. I think he realized that it wouldn't be politically prudent to come out and say this directly, so he couched his criticism by going after a TV sitcom instead. (Sadly, the times have changed sufficiently in the period since the Quayle speech, and now taking such a stand wouldn't be imprudent at all. In fact, it would probably be a sure-fire way to get applause—and votes.)

Pardon me for leading you on this long excursion into Murphy Brown country. I did so to demonstrate that talking about "family values" is an enterprise fraught with peril. It tends to elicit unspoken assumptions, logical non sequiturs, disingenuous statements, and what used to be called bad faith. More than that, it tends to promulgate attitudes of divisiveness ("We have family values and you don't") and *blame*—things that I don't believe are at all helpful if our goal is to increase the well-being of American children, mothers, fathers, families, and society.

I think we can all agree that a "traditional" family, with a mother, a father, one or more children, and a comfortable income is (or can be) a wonderful thing indeed. It is still better if all the people involved are good, generous, and moral, go to church or synagogue each week, don't eat too many sweets, and in their spare time help the homeless and create breathtaking sculptures out of old garden tools. If the income is comfortable enough that one of the parents can stay home to keep the house in order and spend quality and *quantity* time with the children, well, you've hit the jackpot. And no one will complain if, in keeping with long-standing societal norms, the parent who enthusiastically agrees to stay home is the mom.

It's when the real-life examples start diverging from such ideal cases that we start to get in trouble. We live in a very real, very far from ideal, world, and, for one reason or another, just about every family in the country fails to live up to the standards outlined above. What do our "family values" lead us to make of these laggards? It's a trickier question than it might first appear.

Take two phenomena that have occurred over the last thirty years or so and that have been dealt with at length elsewhere in this book: the rise in divorce rates and the large-scale entry of women into the workplace. Both have tended to move the family away from the "ideal" state described above. Yet too often discussions of the negative consequences of those changes for the family (and negative consequences there are) devolve into casting blame on the people (women, usually) who have taken part in them. The term one often hears is "selfish," the idea being that people (women, usually) who pursue careers or decide to leave unhappy marriages are putting their own interests first, at the expense of their children's and, by extension, the institutions of marriage and the family and the entire well-being of society.

It makes sense until you think about it. The implicit, and sometimes explicit, contrast to the "selfishness" of today is the supposed harmony and consensus of the 1950s, when, by and large, husbands and wives stayed together till death did them part and, by and large, mothers did not work outside the home. Yet, as I think I have made clear, this era of good feeling was a historic anomaly, made possible by unique economic and political circumstances, and by the fact that, in general, men held all the economic, social, and political cards. At the time, no one called them selfish. All of a sudden, when things become a little more equalized between the sexes—and when many mothers who would otherwise choose not to are *forced* to work for financial reasons—the accusing cry goes out. Needless to say, a return to the fifties would also mean a return to the days when gays were in the closet, when a couple like Julie and Ellen, whom we met in the last chapter, would not be able to become parents. Some people would welcome such a change; I think it would be a tragedy.

Many of the politicians and theorists who bemoan family decline and advocate a return to traditional ways claim that they do not want to force women back into the home or into unhappy marriages, that they do not want to force gays back into the closet. Yet that would be the unmistakable effect of the changes they advocate. Some, like David Popenoe, the author of *Disturbing the Nest: Family Change and Decline in Modern Societies* and one of the leading voices of the family-values movement, are more frank about their underlying agendas. Popenoe and others decry what they call "androgyny," the notion that mothers and fathers can and quite possibly should perform roughly the same tasks in childrearing, and broadly speaking, the notion that the differences between men and women are mainly instilled by society, not nature.

"Our general view, enforced by constant feminist harangue, is that daddies can make good mommies," he told an interviewer. "It's a mistake—I don't think men are fully cut out for the task. Basically, the woman is the nurturer, the man is the encourager. Woman favors the expressive, man the instrumental. Basically, although the mother may not have a kind of maternal instinct, after the child is born, all sorts of hormonal changes take effect, which biologically induce her to bond with the child. By and large, women are more able to decipher the needs of infants. My view is that it's better for the woman in most cases to stay at home with the infant for the first year or eighteen months, with tremendous help from men. After eighteen months, men and women become much more substitutable."

My view is that this is nonsense. Other than a woman's ability to give birth to and to nurse her baby, there is nothing biological that makes her a better "mommy" than a man could be—that is, if men had the interest, inclination, and social pressure to do so. And the necessity of the mother being on hand 'round the clock for the first eighteen months? Well, if you really want to be "traditional," hark back to premodern times, when infant mortality was so high that babies weren't even *named* until they were two years old, and when upper-class families farmed their babies out to wet nurses as a matter of course. No, human beings have absolutely nothing in their genetic makeup dictating that mom has to be the one.

But even if we wanted to return to the family system of the fifties, that would be an impossible task. So much has happened since then—in terms of changes in the economy, and in men's and women's expectations, in the recognition of gay people as legitimate members of society—that such a return would be, in the words of family sociologist Judith Stacey, "like putting the genie back in the bottle." As much as they may bemoan it, Popenoe and his colleagues won't be able to make a dent in the "androgyny" they perceive. (Others might call it "equality.") The same goes for divorce. Sociologist Andrew Cherlin writes, "We can no more keep wives at home or slash the divorce rate than we can shut down our cities and send everyone back to the farm."

Social movements such as we have witnessed in the last thirty-odd years are far bigger than any group of individuals. They are like the current of a mighty river. You cannot turn it back; all you can hope to do is be aware of it, and channel it in the direction you think would be most advantageous. So the exhortations of family-values politicians, insofar as they call on people to go against the tide, are so much hot air. They might cause a little bit of guilt, and a great deal of divisiveness, but not much more.

And the fact is, despite all the gloom-and-doom talk, the American family—at least the middle-class American family—is not in all that bad a shape. In the last chapter, I detailed some of the ways it has adapted and responded to new pressures, as fathers and grandparents have stepped up their roles, and untraditional kinds of families have come to the fore. In the following chapters, I will describe some of the support the family is (and could be) getting, from government, business, nonprofit support groups, and sources as diverse as computer bulletin boards and agricultural extension agents.

There are all kinds of pressures these days, but the deep-down, underlying values are surprisingly strong. A poll conducted recently for the Mass Mutual Life Insurance Company found that 66 percent of the respondents were "very" or "extremely" satisfied with their own family life. Interestingly, 57 percent felt that the "family life of Americans in general" was "fair" or "poor"—suggesting that if everybody based their perception of the American family on their own family, rather than on media representations or politicians' speeches, there would be a lot less wringing of hands and gnashing of teeth.

Esther Klein, a pollster who conducted a similar survey for *Redbook* magazine, said, "One of the most important changes we found is that the hardships of family life are increasingly external." In other words, the family values are all right, it's just the family circumstances that are a problem: Meals are rushed, the monthly budget doesn't always balance, life in general is hectic, there just doesn't seem to be enough *time* for everything. In fact, the indications were that basic feelings about the family were *improving*, especially in terms of extended family ties. The *Redbook* poll found that the majority of mothers and fathers believe their children have better relationships with grandparents, aunts, and uncles than they did. And 45 percent of the women and 34 percent of the men reported that they were closer to their siblings than their parents were to theirs.

In fact, if you know where to look, the signs are everywhere that middle-class Americans, far from being selfish and hedonistic, are intensely concerned with their families. The fastest-selling category of vehicle is the family minivan. *Every* major hotel chain is instituting family vacation plans. *Family Journal* is a hot new magazine, and children's books are the fastest-growing category in the publishing industry. And any builder who builds a new house without a large family room as the downstairs focus is taking his financial life in his hands.

Even David Blankenhorn, the author of *Fatherless America: Confronting Our Most Urgent Social Problem,* and a leader, along with David Popenoe, of the family-values movement, says, "In general, two-parent families are doing quite well. This generation of fathers is a pretty good group of guys. They're emotionally expressive, communicative, egalitarian. They hug their children a lot and tell them that they love them, as opposed to the handshake model."

You'll notice that I have been referring to the basic health of the "middle-class American family." My phrasing was deliberate. As we move down the economic ladder, the family's conditions and prospects become increasingly bleak. The high out-of-wedlock birthrate among poor Americans—especially poor black Americans—is the most obvious indication of this. (The Murphy Brown Speech and imbroglio notwithstanding, there are proportionately very few middle-class and professional women who are choosing to have children without benefit of marriage.) Leaving aside one's moral, philosophical, or religious feelings about the superiority of the two-parent family, a single-parent home is obviously a handicap in practical terms for a poor child. In addition to starting out with fewer resources than a middle-class counterpart, he or she has to get by with roughly half the personpower, love, interactions, and financial resources of someone in a two-parent home. And all of a sudden the handicap gets a whole lot bigger.

The $64,000 question is, Why has the out-of-wedlock birthrate grown so precipitously among poor people? And the bigger question is, What can be done to address it? Alas, I don't have the definitive answer for either. I don't think anybody does. But I do feel fairly certain that pep talks or lectures to the people involved, exhortations that they take more responsibility for their lives, show more respect for the institution of marriage, abstain from sexual intercourse until marriage, etc., etc.—in short, that they adopt better family values—will accomplish next to nothing. I will go into this further in Chapter VII, "What the Government Can Do for the American Family," but I will say here that punitive measures such as cutting welfare benefits to single mothers will not help, either. In fact, I'm convinced that such measures will be deeply destructive.

No, as with divorce, these trends are bigger than any individual, and any appeals to guilt or conscience or inspiration or even self-interest are not likely to change them in any significant way. Also as with divorce, my suspicion is that the biggest factors responsible for them are economic. It is no accident that the dramatic increase in out-of-wedlock birthrates came just as employment and advancement prospects for inner-city youths had begun to look bleaker than they have ever been before. Being poor is one thing; losing all hope of breaking out of poverty is another. As Elijah Anderson points out, getting married and having a family is a sort of vote of confidence in the future. Should we be surprised that youths with no societal support and few prospects of any kind have declined to cast such a vote?

Nor should we be surprised that they are sexually active. Young people *are* sexually active; it is a fact of social life. In some eras (as in the fifties) they get married early, which tends to legitimize their sexual activity. In some eras (as in the late sixties and seventies) they make frequent use of contraception, which tends to eliminate the consequences of their sexual activity. And in some eras, as in the AIDS epidemic of the eighties and nineties, there are external factors that tend to put a damper on sexual activity. Very rarely do young people change their sexual behavior as a result of public-relations campaigns such as are forthcoming from the family-values supporters.

Do not misunderstand me. I support and applaud the people

and programs that are attempting to instill a sense of sexual responsibility in young people, that are teaching them that actions have consequences and encouraging them to consider abstinence as a viable option. I also support the efforts of people like President Clinton, who see themselves as more than "policy wonks" but as true "leaders" in the traditional sense of the term—individuals who attempt to inspire others to "do the right thing." But I am somewhat skeptical about the effectiveness of all these efforts. I am still more dubious about rhetoric and programs that stigmatize the behavior we would like to change. This is especially counterproductive when they focus, as they so often do, on single *mothers,* forgetting that it takes two to tango. In many cases, in fact, teenaged girls are impregnated by men in their twenties and thirties who, needless to say, take little or no responsibility for the child.

Yes, we need the positive role models and the bully pulpiteering coming from politicians and leaders of all political stripes; in this regard, I think that the obvious family devotion and loyalty shown by President Clinton and Vice President Gore (and President Bush and Vice President Quayle, for that matter) have been very beneficial for the national mood regarding families. We also need the constant reminders—at home, in school, and on the airwaves—that having a baby is an extremely difficult, demanding, time-consuming, messy, and expensive endeavor that can throw a serious monkey wrench in any life or career plans you might have.

But we also need widespread education about and access to contraceptives, and we also must have the right to abortions. The former will reduce the demand for the latter. In virtually every other Western country, teenagers have fewer out-of-wedlock births and fewer abortions than they do in the United States. This is not because they have less sex, but because contraceptives and sex education are widely available.

Even more important, we need to take political and economic steps to see to it that, not too many generations from now, young people in our cities do have realistic hopes of advancing up the economic ladder. That will do more to instill family values than a million speeches.

*   *   *

Let me return to the "middle-class family" for a few moments. (I put the phrase in quotes because I'm not certain it exists, as a single homogeneous entity. But it's a useful concept for argument's sake.) I don't want to leave you with the impression that I think that everything is peaches and cream. I am concerned about what high divorce rates and out-of-wedlock birthrates say about the institution of marriage. Author David Murray writes, "Cultures differ in many ways, but all societies that survive are built on marriage. Marriage is a society's cultural infrastructure, its bridge of social connectedness. The history of human society shows that when people stop marrying, their continuity as a structure is in jeopardy." Murray may be overstating matters a tad (and, I hasten to point out, people in America today have *not* stopped marrying), but he makes a good deal of sense.

By the same token, the large-scale entry of mothers into the workforce has, in general terms, had a negative effect on the welfare of children. "In the very old days, both parents were at home, the children were always underfoot," says my friend and fellow former Israeli Amitai Etzioni, a professor of political science at George Washington University and the founder and chairman of the Communitarian Network. "With industrialization, the father left for the workplace. By definition, that created a deficiency—less parenting. Then more than half the *mothers* left the home for the workplace— replaced by au pair girls and underpaid workers. If I were making shoes and had three million workers, then half of them left, I would have an employee deficit. It's the same way with families— we have a parenting deficit."

True. But I don't think it's particularly useful to address these problems in terms of "values." Simply put, that kind of talk puts the onus on individuals, when the problem really is society's. Among Western countries, we are perhaps the most child- and family-unfriendly. Our businesses tend to be stingy and inflexible in terms of flex time, maternity and paternity leave, and other family policies. Aside from a rather paltry tax deduction for dependents, our government makes virtually no acknowledgment of the difficulty and the importance of raising a family. (In fact, it imposes a marriage *penalty* on couples, forcing them to pay more tax than if they were single and filing separately. It also too often looks the other way when it comes to enforcing the financial obligations of divorced parents.) And our economy finds it appropriate to place child-care workers, one of our most vital human resources, on the very bottom of the salary scale.

So family values are not a problem of any of us; they are a problem of *all* of us.

Fortunately, some voices out there are trying to bolster the family and children, without pointing fingers, casting blame, or attempting (or claiming it is possible) to turn back the clock. One of these is Penelope Leach, the British child-care expert, whose latest book, *Children First,* argues for a fundamental turnabout in society's attitude toward family and children. I read an interview with Leach in *Parents Express,* a Philadelphia monthly, that impressed me so much I clipped it.

Leach was asked to describe her ideal world for parents and children:

> I think it would start from everybody recognizing that bringing up children is a job that is vital to everybody, not just the individual parent. It would start from an acceptance that whatever else is important for people to do in life—earning a living, having a good time and self-fulfillment—that parenting children has to be right up there with the most important of them. . . .
>
> This does not mean in my ideal world every mom would sit at home caring for her child while all the dads went out and earned money for them. . . . We need plenty of shared care for children—it's so all over the world, it's really only here in the West that we have ever had this image of mothers and children shut up together in apartments. I think it's important to stress that while a mother or a father can certainly meet all the needs of a six-month baby, no six-month baby

can meet the much more complicated needs of an adult. And what's more, it isn't a baby's job to do that.

We've grown away from the networks that used to support child care. They were largely female networks, but they needn't have been—the extended family, the neighbors were included, too. You know, the Africans have a saying—in fact, Hillary Clinton used it as the title of a 1996 book—"It takes a village to raise a child."

I'd like us to say: Okay, we haven't got that anymore. And we've tried the nuclear '50s family, and that didn't work too well—women in particular didn't like it a bit. We could make on purpose other kinds of networks that have nothing to do with blood, but are to do with recognizing the need for very young children to be in one-on-one relationships with familiar people. . . .

We have to get male parents thinking as parents. We've now got women almost totally absorbed into what used to be the male work place, but we're nothing like as far in getting men back the other way. And we have to. Women's double burden is not a joke.

Without fathers, parents can't win. In terms of hard practicalities, you have to realize that most businesses are still headed by men. So, until you get men thinking like fathers, they aren't going to want to do it.

Amitai Etzioni and his Communitarian Network are also putting forth some very provocative and worthwhile ideas. One movement they are supporting is an attempt to strengthen the institution of marriage by putting speed bumps on the road to divorce. Etzioni advocates what he calls supervows—"premarital contracts," as he describes them, "in which those about to be betrothed declare they are committing more to their marriage than the law requires. They may choose from a menu of items what they wish to incorporate in their voluntary agreement. For instance, if one spouse requests marital counseling, the other promises to participate. If one asks for a divorce, he or she promises to wait at least six months to see if differences can be worked out."

This is intriguing, although I'm not sure that very many people (especially people with children) get divorced as frivolously as Etzioni seems to think. But I have no objection to running the idea up the flagpole and seeing if anyone salutes: I am in favor of anything that, in a non-finger-pointing way, aims to get people to take the family more seriously. Etzioni's communitarian group has done a great deal in this regard. As its name implies, the organization is a nonpartisan group that seeks to reemphasize the importance of mutual support, respect, and interaction among Americans. Among those who endorsed its "platform" are HUD Secretary Henry Cisneros, pioneer feminist Betty Friedan, conservative theorist Francis Fukuyama, former attorney general Elliot Richardson, and Baltimore mayor Kurt L. Schmoke. As the platform states, "A communitarian perspective recognizes that the preservation of individual liberty depends on the active maintenance of the institutions of civil society where citizens learn respect for one another as well as self-respect; where we acquire a lively sense of our personal and civic responsibilities, along with an appreciation of our rights and the rights of others; where we develop the skills of self-government as well as the habit of governing ourselves, and learn to serve others—not just self."

I think they are right on target in emphasizing the lost importance of community, of which the family, as they point out, is the centerpiece. From my days in the children's home in Switzerland, and the kibbutz in Israel, I know the value of taking responsibility for others as well as yourself, and I agree that community values in America could use a revitalization.

A related group is the Council on Families in America, which includes such notables as authors Sylvia Ann Hewlett, Judith Martin ("Miss Manners"), and William Raspberry; scholars Jean Bethke Elshtain, Mary Ann Glendon, Leon R. Kass, Martin Marty, and Judith Wallerstein; White House aide William A. Galston; and family therapist Theodora Ooms. The council recently offered eight "propositions" on the family in America. While I don't agree with all of them (in particular, I think they are a little too gloomy on the current state of the family, and a little too adamant about the superiority of the two-parent model, to the exclusion of all other alternatives), I think they are a step in the right direction, and I think they deserve to be quoted at length:

1. In order to develop emotionally, socially and morally, a child requires a strong, warm, lasting, and loving attachment with at least one and preferably two or more adults who are deeply committed to that child's well-being.

2. A basic social purpose of the family is to rear children to become adults who are self-confident, socially responsible, and capable of attachment and trust. The family, in short, carries the key social and moral responsibility for raising the next generation.

3. Today the family is in a crisis that fundamentally threatens the well-being of our nation's children. The marriage bond is steadily weakening. Indeed, marriage is becoming deinstitutionalized. Children are spending less time with their parents, especially their fathers. Across the society, children are less valued. . . .

4. The current disintegration of the well-functioning, two-parent family is a central cause of rising individual and social pathology. . . . The evidence is strong and growing that the current generation of children and youth is the first in our nation's history to be less well-off—psychologically, socially, economically, and morally—than their parents were at the same age.

5. Family ties were relatively strong in the "traditional nuclear family," with its strict social roles of male breadwinner and female homemaker. . . . Today, because of the importance of female equality and the changing conditions of modern society, that previous model of life-long, separate-sphere gender roles is no longer desirable or possible on a society-wide scale.

6. Yet the model of the two-parent family, based on a lasting, monogamous marriage, remains both possible and desirable. Considering all the alternatives, this family form is by far the most efficacious one for children and for long-term individual and societal well-being.

7. The characteristics of an ideal social environment for child-rearing consists of an enduring, two-biological-parent family that

engages regularly in activities together; has many of its own routines, traditions, and stories; and provides a great deal of contact between adults and children. The children have frequent interaction with relatives, with neighbors in a supportive neighborhood, and with their parents' world of work, coupled with no pervasive worry that their parents will break up. Finally, each of these ingredients comes together in the development of a rich family subculture that has lasting meaning and strongly promulgates such family values as responsibility, honesty, cooperation, and sharing. . . .

8. A major cultural and policy imperative for our time is to increase the proportion of children who grow up with their two married parents and to decrease the proportion of children who do not.

As you read the last point—and, indeed, the entire statement—I can almost hear a one-word question being asked by most readers: How? And the fact is, even if we unanimously agree on what our "family values" should be (hardly a sure thing), the matter of transmitting those values to the American public is vexing in the extreme. Of course, the usual way people in our society are persuaded to adopt new ideas, opinions, tastes, and even values is by advertising or public-relations campaigns, and this has some relevance here.

Don't laugh. What was Dan Quayle's speech but the first sally of a PR campaign, aimed at putting across his particular view of the family? Every prominent person with a strong view on the issue—whether Al Gore, David Blankenhorn, Amitai Etzioni, or yours truly—understands that it is not possible to legislate people into *thinking* a certain way, and the attempt to legislate them into *behaving* in certain ways is fraught with peril. (I will discuss this at greater length in Chapter VII, "What the Government Can Do for the American Family.") So we all take to the stump, whether in the form of speeches, books, op-ed pieces, or television interviews, thinking that our eloquence and the underlying wisdom of our ideas will inspire Americans to reshape their vision of their own families, that their examples will inspire their neighbors, co-workers, and relatives, and so on down the line. In politics, this is known as the "bully pulpit," and it can be a tool of some, though hardly overwhelming, effectiveness. President Clinton has certainly attempted to use it in regard to the family, vowing in his 1995 State of the Union Address to enlist parents, religious organizations, and community groups in a national campaign against "our most serious social problem, the epidemic of teen pregnancies and births where there is no marriage."

But this kind of effort is far from sufficient. By and large, no amount of speechifying is going to make a significant change in values, family values included. As a matter of fact, if our basic values regarding the family are as far gone as some of the alarmists claim they are, there's little hope for us. But I believe that our underlying values are sound, and that, when all the rhetoric and finger-pointing and politicking are cleared away, we are in general agreement on these matters—or, at least, in close enough agreement that we can proceed to the real work at hand. What's needed, in short, is a *practical* approach.

And so, in the remainder of the book, I am going to accentuate the practical. (I *always* accentuate the positive.) In the next chapter, I will describe concrete steps that are currently being taken to help the family; the good news here is that there is more exciting stuff going on, I would wager, than even the most well informed of you are aware of. After that, I will share with you some of my thoughts on the most promising directions for action—in the governmental, corporate, and personal sphere—as we approach the year 2000.

Chapter VI

What's Being Done to Help the American Family?

There are strollers, cribs, toys, and baby clothes all over the place in the airy office suite, and a couple of volunteers sorting them out. The shelves are crammed with kids' books, games, and parenting guides. On the wall is a signed photo from Charlotte Lopez, Miss Teen USA 1993. The light-filled, glassed-in play area is filling up with kids, and the phone keeps ringing. A heavy mom with very long, straight, blond hair arrives for the weekly Mothers' Group with her two little blond girls.

"How are you?" she is asked.

"Pregnant," she replies.

One of the little girls, who looks to be about five and is obviously concerned about the prospect of acquiring yet another sister, says, "When I grow up, I'm going to have a boy and a girl."

It's a typical morning at the Center for Kids and Family in Toms River, New Jersey. The center, which is directed by an energetic woman named Kathy Palomara, was started about six years ago, Palomara says, when the Community Medical Center, a local hospital, "decided to expand the definition of health care." So they gave Palomara (at that point there was no staff) some office space adjoining the hospital, a phone line, a modest budget, and the mission to do whatever she could manage to help Ocean County families.

Since then the center has grown to an enterprise with six full-time staffers, a slew of volunteers, 20,000 members in the community, and a dizzying array of services. Some of them are directly related to the hospital. For example, the center will provide up to two hours of free child care for anyone using hospital service.

But others reach far into the outside world. There is a twenty-four-hour family-issue hot line that gets about 1,200 calls a month. The people who answer the phone—trained health-care professionals—use a computer database program, so that when they input the problem for which they can't fully respond from their own knowledge and training—say, alcohol abuse—they see a list of resources: organizations, books, support groups.

There are also:

• infant-care classes for first-time parents, and a Parenting Skills Workshop for parents of older children, both with modest fees;
• a "Safe Sitter Program," a short course designed to give baby-sitters the basics of child care and emergency management, and "You Hold the Key," a program designed to help and instruct kids who are alone after school;
• a lending library of books, videos, and other resources, including the center's own self-published book, *Balancing Work and Home—Tip and Recipe Book*;
• Parents Anonymous, a weekly support group "for parents to share their experiences in a non-judgmental atmosphere";
• a monthly support group for parents of children with Attention Deficit Disorder;
• a program to lend a car seat to any family that asks for one, and to provide cribs, toys, clothing, and other baby supplies to needy families.

And that is not all. "We do a lot of workshops on balancing work and home," says Palomara, who knows her way all around this particular issue, being mother to five kids between the ages of five and thirteen—three of her own and two of her sister's children of whom she has custody. "One of the exercises is to have people rank their priorities, then to go through their appointment books to see if they are practicing what they preach. We'll say, 'You said that family was your first priority, but it's way down the list.' We'll have them *schedule* family time in their books. And we try to work with them to recognize when their standards aren't realistic, like when women think their houses have to be immaculate. I'll say, 'Did you ever read on a tombstone, "This was the best housekeeper ever"?' "

The center also provides four- to five-week parenting education for moms and dads whom the state Division of Youth and Family Services decides are in need of counseling or training because, for example, they are potentially abusive. In cooperation with the local prosecutor, it does a violence-prevention program in the schools, five two-hour sessions that teach kids about avoiding the impulse to fight and trying to negotiate solutions to their problems.

From behind her desk, Palomara pulls out a strikingly realistic, life-sized baby doll. "It's called Baby Think It Over," she says. "It was developed by a rocket scientist in California who had been laid off. We use it in family-life classes in the schools. It weighs about twenty pounds, and a microchip makes it start crying at unannounced intervals—including during the night, of course. The only way to stop it is to hold it between five and thirty-five minutes. A teenager will take it home for the weekend, and when she brings it back, the chip will tell the instructor how long the student took to pick it up, and also whether she was abusive."

At $300, the doll obviously doesn't make sense as a birthday gift for a five-year-old. But for its intended audience, it seems well worth the price; it might single-handedly do more to reduce the teen pregnancy rate than any number of family-planning seminars. (According to newspaper accounts, the scientist/inventor, Rick Jurmain, got the idea shortly after watching a television program about teenagers carrying around "baby" flour sacks. "That's not very good," he commented to his wife. "It doesn't cry, and it doesn't wake you up in the middle of the night." A few weeks later *he* woke his wife up in the middle of the night and told her he had the idea for Baby Think It Over.)

The phone rings, as it's been doing all morning. "This is the Center for Kids and Family," Palomara says. "May I help you? . . . We'll have to put you on a waiting list for a car seat. You can come in anytime for clothes."

One of the center's popular programs—and the one that the blond mother/mother-to-be is here for this morning—arose, Palomara says, "when we started getting a lot of calls from moms saying, 'I feel so discriminated against. People resent the fact that I'm staying home with my kids. I need a place to meet and talk with other people like me.' So we started a Mothers' Support Group. (We changed the name to 'Mothers' Group' because the word *support* made it sound too much like they were victims.) We provide child care, and there are about fifteen to twenty of them who come in every week. They're from all different backgrounds—we have an attorney and a single mother in the same group."

My intention is not to nominate Kathy Palomara and the Center for Kids and Family for the Nobel Prize. They have not hit upon some earth-shattering secrets to solving America's family problems, nor are they the only group offering these kinds of services. And that, in fact, *is* the point I want to make. The Center for Kids and Family is just one of *thousands* of family-support programs going on around the country. Some are all-in-one one-stop-shopping family resource facilities, like the Center for Kids and Family; others focus on a particular service or need. Some are long standing and well endowed; others are just getting off the ground and are operating on a shoestring. Some are funded exclusively by private money, some by public, and some by a combination. Some are independent; others are sponsored by churches, hospitals, schools, day-care centers, or universities. But they are all out there working to help the family, in a nonideological, nuts-and-bolts, roll-up-your-sleeves-and-lend-a-hand manner. And, far more than any amount of hot air emanating from Washington (or Cambridge, New Haven, or Princeton, for that matter), they provide the model we're going to have to follow if we are to solve our family problems.

I have a personal involvement with and therefore firsthand

knowledge of one national program—the Home Instruction Program for Preschool Youngsters, more commonly known as HIPPY. The involvement stems from the fact that my daughter, Miriam, is the executive director. The program started in Israel in the late sixties under the leadership of Avima Lombard, and, as its name implies, is intended to train parents of three- to five-year-olds, at home, to help give their children a better head start when they begin school.

Interestingly, HIPPY was designed to provide a contrast to the early Head Start programs, which, Miriam says, "had an unintended outcome—giving parents the message that the earlier the kid got out of the house, the better off they'd be. It internalized helplessness. Head Start is different today—it stresses home-based efforts. As a matter of fact, several Head Start centers do HIPPY programs."

HIPPY came to America about ten years ago and now oversees more than 100 programs around the country, serving about 13,000 people. (More of them—some 5,000 families served by 30 programs—are in Arkansas than any other state. This is because one of HIPPY's most ardent advocates is a former Arkansas first lady, someone by the name of Hillary Rodham Clinton. In 1991, she pushed a bill called the Better Chance Program Act, specifically designed to provide funding for HIPPY and similar programs.) Half of the programs operate through schools or preschools; the other half through community-based organizations—Y's, churches, job-training centers, and so forth. They're all funded differently—through federal grants, state grants, funding sources within schools (such as Title I for at-risk kids), Head Start, a federal program called Even Start. The one constant is that parents do not pay.

The parent-training is done by paraprofessionals who themselves go through an intensive training program administered through the national office. After that, they are assigned twelve to fifteen families, meeting with them every other week.

"In the first year of a program," Miriam says, "recruitment [of families] is difficult. From the second year on, typically, there is a waiting list." And why shouldn't there be? The families recognize

135

what scholarly studies are now beginning to confirm: that kids with HIPPY do better in first-grade classrooms than non-HIPPY children. Significantly, HIPPY also improves mothers' self-esteem, involvement in their children's education, and interest in their *own* further education.

I don't want my parental pride to give the impression that HIPPY is the only program that attempts to promote literacy and education by way of the family. There are many. I asked Secretary of Education Richard Riley to share with me a few of the ones he has been particularly impressed with, and I'd like to pass them on to you.

The **School Development Program**, founded by Dr. James P. Comer, a professor of psychiatry at Yale, is designed to change the climate of schools that primarily serve disadvantaged children, making them more responsive to the needs of the students and their families. One of the ways it does so is both by involving parents in the decision-making process and seeing that they share in the responsibility for those decisions. The **MegaSkills Program**, developed by Dr. Dorothy Rich and now serving some 65,000 families in 45 states, engages parents and community volunteers to help children acquire—at home—skills and attitudes that are linked to successful school performance. These are the "megaskills": confidence, motivation, effort, responsibility, initiative, perseverance, caring, teamwork, common sense, and problem solving.

Those are national programs. On a state level, according to Secretary Riley, one exemplary operation is Missouri's fifteen-year-old **Parents as Teachers** (PAT) program. Designed to strengthen families' roles in fostering children's development and learning, it includes home visits, group meetings for parents, regular monitoring of children's health and developmental status, and referral to social-service and other agencies when necessary. A parent educator visits participating families at least four times a year, and implements a home curriculum based on the work of Dr. Burton White and Dr. T. Berry Brazelton.

*   *   *

HIPPY and the other programs I've just discussed all focus on education; of course, there are many others with different emphases. It's a near-impossible task to keep track of them all, so I give thanks for the Family Resource Coalition, founded in 1981 and headquartered in Chicago. It is the nerve center for the family-support movement, providing research, technical assistance and training, government liaison, and just plain moral support for more than 2,500 diverse programs around the country.

As with HIPPY, underpinning all the efforts of the Family Resource Coalition has been the belief that *parents* are the most important factors in a child's life and development. In other words, these programs aren't designed just to swoop in and "save" kids in some magical way, brushing their mothers and fathers aside. From the coalition's early days, it operated on the principle that, in the words of its founder, Bernice Weissbourd, "a parent's feelings about her- or himself was absolutely primary to how that parent would relate to the child—that it was really off base to think that you could expect a child to develop a feeling of self-confidence and competence when the parent was feeling depressed and ineffectual. We felt that the need to feel competent cut across economic and racial lines, and we wanted to have a program that would build *parents'* capacities."

The coalition defines the following components as typical of a family-support program:

• Life skills training. This may include family literacy, education, employment or vocational training, or enhancement of personal development skills such as problem solving, stress reduction, and communication.

• Parent information classes and support groups. These provide instruction in child development and opportunities for parents to share their experiences and concerns with their peers.

• Parent-child groups and family activities, which provide occasions for parents to spend more time with their children.

• Drop-in time to provide parents with informal opportunities to spend time with staff members and other parents.

• Information and referral services.

• Crisis intervention/family counseling to respond to parents' special concerns about their children or specific family issues.

• Auxiliary support services such as clothing exchanges, emergency food, transportation.

If you're interested in contacting the Family Resource Coalition—either for information on programs in your area or for assistance in starting or running a program—the organization is located at: 200 South Michigan Avenue, Suite 1520, Chicago, Illinois 69694. The telephone number is 312-341-0900.

As I say, there are thousands and thousands of family-support programs throughout the country—far too many for me to describe or even list here. What I can and will do, however, is highlight a few of the programs, plucked to show the array of approaches, services, and methods that are out there.

• I'll start in my own neighborhood, the Washington Heights section of Manhattan. At Intermediate School 218, the Children's Aid Society sponsors the **Children's Aid Program,** a "full-service" school that's designed to be the center of community life, where people work together to solve their problems. The school is open from 7:00 A.M. to 10:00 P.M. and provides a location where families can obtain the services of social workers, dentists, and nurses, as well as classes in such diverse subjects as aerobics, English as a second language, and the college preparatory curriculum. The **Young Men's and Young Women's Hebrew Association's Center,** also in Washington Heights (for whom I've served as a board member since 1970 and as president for the past five years), has a full range of activities for the support and recreational needs of families in the community. I have also been involved in the creation of and fundraising efforts for Kennedy Airport's **Kidsport Day Care Center,** where employees can enroll their children. The hours at the center have been extended to accommodate the needs of parents and their children.

• In Chester, Pennsylvania, **Single Mothers Raising Sons** is a support group for women in this poor, predominantly black city near Philadelphia. Founded in 1994 by Reuben Guy, a social worker with Catholic Social Services, the group provides mutual support to women who want to talk to their sons about the painful subject of fathers who have been lost to death, divorce, jail, or indifference. The group helps the women negotiate the community-services labyrinth as well and has helped them obtain housing, offered legal assistance for child support, and conducted classes toward the goal of receiving a General Equivalency Diploma.

• In Cleveland, an organization called the **Institute for Responsible Fatherhood and Family Revitalization** has addressed the other side of the problem, working to reconnect more than 2,000 absent fathers with their children. Director Charles Ballard believes that if men are convinced of the importance of being good fathers, they will become motivated to finish school and find work. A study of the program by two Case Western Reserve professors bears him out: It found that 97 percent of the men began providing financial support for their children, 71 percent had not had any more children at the time of the study, and 62 percent of the previously unemployed men found full-time work.

• The **Generations Together** program, at the University of Pittsburgh, brings together children and older people in a kind of "adopt-a-grandparent" program. They interact not only individually but in group settings. Thus, at Pittsburgh's High School for the Performing Arts, elder "artists in residence" pass their creative skills on to students. And at the Eastern District Area School for Exceptional Living, volunteers work with the emotionally disturbed and disabled students.

• **Denver Family Opportunity** (DFO) is a welfare-to-jobs program that emphasizes the family. A participant discusses employment plans with a caseworker only after a very full family assessment, designed to elicit information on parenting, educational process of children, family violence, housing needs, and the availability of support networks. Through interagency agreements and networks, DFO can connect participants to a wide range of educational, health, training, legal, and other services. In addition, it provides, on site, a drop-in child-care center so parents can work on their job strategy, developmental screening for children, and housing assistance.

• Tennessee's **Comprehensive Child Development Effort** operates five family resource centers, all affiliated with neighborhood schools, in four rural west Tennessee counties, that are designed to offer comprehensive and intensive services to families in need. In addition to the activities, programs, and workshops at the centers, each participating family receives a weekly ninety-minute home visit by a caseworker. Available services include medical, dental, and prenatal care; adult education; parenting education; housing assistance; employment counseling; and early intervention for at-risk children.

• In northern California, the **Parenting Services Project** grew out of the realization that low- and moderate-income parents using day-care centers were likely to have family needs beyond just child care, and that the child-care center was an excellent, nonthreatening entry point for offering such families—many of whom spoke little or no English—the assistance they needed. Under PSP, child-care centers were transformed into *family* care centers; today services are provided to more than 2,000 families, with parenting classes, peer support groups, job training, sick-child care, family-fun events, and referrals to other community services.

One wonderful resource, as far as family support goes, is the U.S. Department of Agriculture Cooperative Extension Service. For those who associate this unit with agents who come out and test the soil and with the organizing of 4-H clubs, it will come as a surprise to learn that one of its primary purposes is to provide resources that are designed to help families grow, flourish, and deal with their problems.

"Unlike most other agencies, we don't serve a narrow audience," says Charles A. "Chuck" Smith, a human development specialist at the Kansas State University Cooperative Extension Service (the extension service is typically associated with a state's land-grant university). "We deal with the public as a whole, and our mission is to bring education and information to the people on issues of practical concern. Here in Kansas, for example, my colleagues and I at the university will develop parent-education programs, which we will then transmit to extension agents, who work with specific counties. If you want to find your local agent, pick up the local phone book and look under the county government listings for words like *extension council* or *cooperative extension service.*

"We are involved in practically every conceivable issue. We do a lot with after-school care, a lot dealing with the education of teachers of young children. We work with at-risk parents, helping single parents not just in parenting but also money management."

Traditionally, each state extension service has been quite autonomous. Smith, who has been on loan from his university to work as a national program leader in human development, has been making efforts to integrate the extension services. Recently, he and three colleagues—Dorothea Cudaback from the University of California, H. Wallace Goddard from Auburn University, and Judith A. Myers-Walls from Purdue University—published *National Extension Parent Education Model of Critical Parenting Practices*, a short but wonderful book that attempts, as Smith says, "to create a model, to serve as common grounds for all efforts in parent education.

"Although each state is different, there are commonalities: No matter if you are in Bangor, or Austin, or Portland, there are common concerns. We spent a year and a half trying to synthesize approaches and came up with twenty-nine 'priority parent practices,' organized into six categories: Care for Self, Understand, Guide, Nurture, Motivate, and Advocate. In one we did a literature review and tried to summarize the conclusions. Then we included an annotated 'curriculum guide' of available materials, and a chapter giving guidance on how to implement and deliver the various strategies."

I can think of no better place to start for anyone interested in starting a parent-education program than the book, which is available for $10 from: Charles A. Smith, Room 343 Justin Hall,

School of Family Studies and Student Services, Kansas State University, Manhattan, Kansas 66506.

The book has certainly created interest in Washington: I picked up my copy at the vice president's office, where it has been pored over. The White House has also expressed interest in another national project of Smith's.

"I'm convinced that what we have to do to reach parents really in need of support is not write a publication, but find natural helpers who live in a community and get them to volunteer to work with younger parents who are struggling," he explains. "These would be experienced parents, in some cases grandparents, whose children have left home. You spend all this time learning about being a parent, developing a body of knowledge, then the kids go away and you have no one to use it on. We're going to try to pilot the program at sites around the country this year, and the White House has expressed a lot of interest."

Still, most of the Extension Service's work continues to be done on a state or county level. Here are some examples of the exciting programs under way.

• In Colorado, the Colorado State University Cooperative Extension faculty offers **How to Talk So Kids Will Listen**, a self-contained multimedia parenting course, taking place over seven weekly sessions of two hours each and designed to help parents communicate more effectively with their children. In one survey of those who had completed the course, parents reported a significant decrease in family strain levels. One hundred percent reported making one or more behavioral changes as a result of the course, 73 percent reported two or more changes, and 100 percent said they favored continued use of tax dollars to fund this kind of course.

• The University of Massachusetts' **Master Teacher in Family Life Program** works to identify leaders within a community, and then, through a highly refined training program, to provide them with the technical information and critical-thinking skills they need to build their communities, specifically by targeting and helping at-risk youth. The presence of these "Master Teachers" back in the community, the program has found, becomes a galvanizing and unifying force. From its start in 1991, the program has expanded to a national scope. Thus far, its philosophy and methods have been used in forty states: in communities damaged by the 1993 floods, in riot-torn Los Angeles, in a Native American reservation in Wyoming, and in gold-mining communities in Nevada.

• At the University of Missouri, the Extension Service provides a multitude of services targeted to individual businesses under the rubric **Balancing Work and Family**. It will provide on-site workshops for a business's employees; provide books, pamphlets, audiovisual aids, and computer resources on the subject; assist with workplace and community surveys to identify needs and resources; and give technical assistance on specific programs and policies. The service also runs a program called **Talent Ties**, which brings together kids and older adults in one-on-one sessions based on shared interests like photography, computers, or gardening.

• Chuck Smith has designed a workshop for parents called **Responsive Discipline**, with materials organized so that parents who cannot attend may use them as a learn-at-home course. The Kansas State Extension Service also administers **Students Helping Students**, an after-school program that uses at-risk high school students as mentors for elementary school students, and that has achieved some extraordinary results.

Extension Service personnel are also poised to react to specific events. When a natural disaster (like a flood or earthquake) or a man-made disaster (like a plant or army-base closing) occurs, they are ready to come to the aid of the families affected. As a matter of fact, both the Extension Service and the military have lately done some excellent family work, relating both to base closings and the general stress of trying to bring up a family in a military environment. (Domestic abuse and other indicators of family strife are traditionally higher among military families than in the population at large.)

An example of how extension professionals approach such a traumatic event as this comes in the form of an electronic-mail message I picked up one day on Famnet, a computerized mailing list that goes to extension family specialists around the country, as well as to others who work with or are interested in families. It was written by Suzanna Smith, Ph.D., who is both a human development specialist for the Florida Cooperative Extension Service and a professor of human development and family relations at the University of Florida. I was especially interested in the way Dr. Smith, though obviously very knowledgeable in the field, was at the same time eager to reach out for help. This is what she wrote:

In November 1994, citizens of the State of Florida passed a constitutional amendment banning commercial inshore net fishing. This begins July 1, 1995; between 1,500 and 2,000 commercial fishers will be affected. However, the repercussions go much beyond this number. Inshore net fishing is typically a family-based occupation and women and children are often involved. Some communities are organized around fishing, wholesale and retail trade, processing and restaurant sales, so that entire villages will be affected.

We are anticipating that this will be a difficult time for many families. Many fishers are middle-aged, have a high school education and have been fishing since they were teenagers. Many come from fishing families. In some rural areas job prospects are especially limited. Many observers expect that the closer we get to July 1, the more likely we are to see violence, including domestic violence, and other manifestations of distress.

During the next few months, the Florida Cooperative Extension Service (CES) will be developing programs to assist commercial fishing families. CES county and state faculty will be meeting together and with community representatives to determine how we can best respond.

As a Human Development Specialist, I will be responsible for providing materials, consultation and support for county Extension faculty as they work with families and communities on issues such as family stress and coping, conflict, communication, etc. A colleague will be covering family financial concerns.

I do have some experience with these families, having conducted research on the impacts of regulatory changes on commercial fishing families. However, the net ban introduces a whole new set of problems and issues; and it may be difficult to reach this audience through more traditional extension methods. I would greatly appreciate any advice based on similar experience in Canada or other parts of the U.S., print or AV educational materials, models for working with these families and communities, or other resources that might help us to work effectively with this audience to address problems associated with the ban.

There's a lot of government-bashing these days. I, for one, couldn't be prouder to have someone as dedicated, knowledgeable, and (I am certain) as skilled as Dr. Smith as a representative of *my* government.

Rabbi Elliot Strom realized that his training just had not been good enough. Yes, he knew his Torah and his Talmud. But when an engaged couple who were members of his Newtown, Pennsylvania, congregation came to see him one day about a dozen years ago, he understood in a flash of insight that some aspects of the job he was simply not prepared to handle.

"We were talking about the ceremony and they were on each other, squabbling, practically throwing daggers," Rabbi Strom told the *Philadelphia Inquirer*. "It needed to be addressed on a deeper level, and I wasn't equipped."

Thank God for people who realize their limitations and take steps to correct them. Rabbi Strom is one of those people. Soon after his epiphany, he enrolled in a marital-counseling course for clergy offered by the Penn Council for Relationships in Philadelphia. The course, and many others like it around the country, are part of a growing recognition that if we want to bolster the institution of marriage—and, by extension, the family itself—the earlier we start the better, and the more well trained we are the better. And they constitute an important component of the family-support movement.

One organization has long acted in this direction: the Catholic Church. It has been an article of canon law since 1917 that engaged couples must go through some form of marriage preparation. Usually this has taken the form of a "pre-Cana" (that is, "before the feast") workshop that lasts from several hours to a day and consists of groups of couples—both married and soon to be married—talking about the important issues that will face them, from sex to finances, from whose job will take precedence to whose job it will be to take out the garbage.

But the Church, other religious organizations, and some secular groups have taken this idea several steps farther. Today, marriage-preparation programs can take weeks and involve intensive soul-searching and engagement (in *both* senses of the word) among the couples. And why not? We think nothing of taking weeks of training before learning to fly a plane; sustaining a good marriage is infinitely more complicated—and more dangerous.

Many of these programs use an exercise known as PREPARE (Premarital Personal and Relationship Evaluation), developed by social scientist David Olson. It consists of 125 statements; for example, "I expect that some romantic love will fade after marriage" and "I can easily share my positive and negative feelings with my partner." Individuals are asked how strongly they agree or disagree with the statements; based on the responses, Olson says, he can predict with 80 to 85 percent accuracy whether the marriage will end in divorce. Reportedly, 10 percent of the couples break off their engagements when they learn their scores—like a *Scared Straight* for couples-to-be.

An effort that tries to reach people even earlier in their lives is the Preserving Marriages Project, the brainchild of Lynn Gold-Bikin, a Norristown, Pennsylvania, lawyer who chairs the family law division of the American Bar Association. She and other lawyers, all of whom contribute their time, go into high school classrooms around the country and conduct role-playing exercises designed to show

how difficult it can be to maintain a serious relationship. Lest any of the kids think that divorce is painless, Gold-Bikin and her colleagues make very clear the emotional scars, anxiety, and economic costs it can leave in its wake.

Even if I were not a therapist myself, I would be grossly remiss if I did not discuss one of the most significant and wide-ranging institutions in bolstering the American family: the family-therapy profession. Some 4.6 million couples a year visit 50,000 licensed family therapists in this country, up from 1.2 million in 1980. In many cases, of course, it's the entire family that sees the therapist, not just a couple. A measure of how respectable this form of therapy has become is that at the 1992 Democratic National Convention, Vice President Gore said that his family had been in family therapy, and no one batted an eye. Compare that to 1972, when the disclosure of the mental-health treatment received by another Democratic vice presidential candidate, Thomas Eagleton, effectively ended his political career.

I am not a family therapist myself (sex therapy is a very different enterprise, in method as well as focus), but I have long admired my colleagues in this specialty. Such pioneers as Salvador Minuchin, Murray Bowen, and Gregory Bateson have all developed their own schools, but what they have in common is a view of the family being treated as an interlocking, interdependent *system*. Family therapy is called for when, for one reason or another, the system is not functioning properly, when one member's problems reflect dysfunctional interactions in the family as a whole. A skilled therapist will meet with the family, usually in weekly sessions, and, together with them, come to an understanding about its (usually unspoken) assumptions, its "alliances" and "hierarchies," and then attempt to determine how these might be adjusted or restructured in order to increase the health of the family and its members.

It is a form of group therapy, but with an important difference. "In family therapy, we look at groups that are not artificial—that are linked together, that have a history and a language in common," said Salvador Minuchin, the founder of the "structural" school of therapy, in an interview with *Psychology Today*. "In that setting, the therapist still has the power of owning 'knowledge'; he can control communication, when to introduce insight, etc. The family therapist is in a different territory. The people he's seeing enter into the room with alliances, stories that they know that you don't know, secrets and silences."

The family-therapy movement can be blamed for one thing: It introduced the term "dysfunctional family," and thus is at least partly responsible for the excesses of Phil, Oprah, Geraldo, and all the rest. But it is also responsible for helping untold numbers of American families, and that is a far, far more important accomplishment.

I have referred at various points over the course of the book to computer networks, mailing lists, bulletin boards, and so forth over which family information is transmitted. I'd like to take a moment now to highlight some of these Internet resources, for I think they are more than simply conduits of information; they are, in themselves, an exciting family support system.

An example of the possibilities inherent in the technology is the work done by Brad and Cathy Furry, operators of the Littlest Unicorn Day Care and Online Resource Center in Kansas City, Missouri. The Furrys have put on-line every licensed child-care provider in the state, searchable by ZIP code, name of center, and city. They also make electronically available files and articles related to family and child-care issues for educators, child-care providers, and parents. Their E-mail address is 73741.343@compuserve. com.

One mailing list that Ben Yagoda, my co-author, subscribes to, with much fascination, is Fathers in Education, which can be reached at father-l@vm1.spcs.umn.edu. The list is designed for fathers to share information, questions, and concerns, so Ben is what the computer people call a "lurker." But the lurking has been fascinating, with all kinds of discussions about every conceivable issue facing fathers. Probably the most interesting one recently was a discussion of the pros and cons of corporal punishment; it went on, with heated, but never angry, arguments back and forth, for a full month.

One "Internet jewel" that Ben downloaded from the Fathers in Education list was a "Guide to Online Resources for Youth and Youth Workers" put together by Kenneth Udut. If anyone wants the whole list, it can be gotten by contacting Mr. Udut at kudut@ritz.mordor.com. He writes, "If you are writing a book on the Internet, I would be honored if you would include this list. You don't need my permission." Here are some of the highlights:

• add-parent@mv.mv.com is a support group for parents of kids with Attention Deficit Disorder.

• *The Child Abuse Handbook,* "designed to provide concise information to help education staff respond to suspected child abuse," can be located on the World Wide Web at http://www.fcbe.edu.on.ca/www/welcome.html.

• *Notes from the Windowsill* is an electronic journal devoted to reviews of children's books. To subscribe, write to kidsbook-request@armory.com, and remember to give your full E-mail address in the body of your letter.

• The National Parent Information Network, described as "a new national resource for parents, families and people who support them," includes short articles on a variety of topics; PARENTS AskERIC, a question-answering service; forums for discussion of common concerns; and listings of useful and readily available materials. You can reach it by gophering to: ericps.ed.uinc.edu, or by finding your way to the World Wide Web site: http://ericps.ed.uinc.edu/npin/npinhome.html.

• The Media Literacy Project is an ongoing research activity at the University of Oregon's College of Education. It administers a gopher service containing all manner of information on the topic. Gopher to: interact.uoregon.edu.

• The Children, Youth and Family discussion group is run out of the University of Minnesota. To subscribe, just E-mail listserv@umnnn1.bitnet and then give the message sub cyf-l Firstname Lastname.

• "Dadvocat" is a cleverly named mailing list intended for fathers of children with disabilities or special health needs. To subscribe, E-mail listserv@ukcc.bitnet and give the message sub dadvocat Firstname Lastname.

• Finally, an intriguing entry that Ben hasn't tried and so can't guarantee, but it sounds fascinating: a software program called Destination: Earth that "simulates growing up in America." "Starts at age 17, in HS, and player/teen has his life before him," writes the creator. "Events happen and decisions need to be made. Covers education, career, finances, social relationships, family and crises (drugs, AIDS). Player chooses personality and social-economic background at game start." This is clearly beyond me, but I encourage my more computer-literate readers to give it a try. Type ftp.indirect.copm/www/gstarman/deread.txt to get Destination: Earth at the ftp site.

I'll close this section with an exchange that I think illustrates both the "high-touch" capability of the supposedly cold high-tech world and also the simple heartwarming value of love of family and person-to-person contact. Someone wrote the Fathers in Education list with this message (all typos retained):

"I am a 19 years old, and my fiance and I are expecting our first baby September 15th. Although this was an unexpected pregnancy, we are most definitely going to take on this responsibility. The only problem I am facing is the knowledge of how to parent a child. It wasn't but a few years ago that I was referred to as a kid myself, and now I am going to raise one. I will read the notes posted through this newsgroup in hopes of learning, and I know that with the help of you all, and your valuable advice, I will be able to do this."

He got this reply:

"Welcome to the final frontier! I don't know what advice you've gotten from others, but it seems to me, from my vast seven years experience, that there is nothing you can read, no course you can take, that will prepare you for the journey. You can learn the practical aspects—how to do things, etc., and prepare to take over a lot of house-hold tasks while Mom deals with breastfeeding and such in the early months, but there is an emotional/spiritual transformation that passes thru a man when he has kids that you can never prepare for. You hang on and ride it out. I think it is a life-affirming, completely enriching experience that I would not trade for anything.

"Some other practical advice: Ask all the questions you want, and ask a lot of people. Everyone has different ideas and tricks they've learned, from your pediatrician to your partner's mother. Accept your own instincts. I know, men aren't supposed to have them, but we do, and they often will steer us in exactly the right direction. If you're feeling uptight and stressed, make some time for yourself. Don't disappear for days, but a night out with the guys can work wonders, especially if you know it is coming and you can look forward to it. Don't ever hit. I've come oh-so-close to smacking mine on many occasions, and I knew that once I did, it would get easier and easier. I felt that it was the only solution at the moment. Walk away, breathe, go outside and scream, run around the block, whatever you have to do to burn off the energy, then go back and face the situation calmly.

"Enjoy each other. I know people say it goes by so fast, and it does. Dont let a day go by without telling your child you love him."

CHAPTER VII

What the Government Can Do for the American Family

By the time you are reading these words, the "Contract with America" may be a distant and hazy memory. But as I write them, the Contract, pledged to by the Republican Party as it took control of the Senate and the House of Representatives in 1995, is a nearly ubiquitous concept that is believed to represent a sea of change in American politics, values, and life.

Ask anyone (certainly any Republican) what the Contract represents, and I'll bet that one of the first things he or she says is "family." Indeed, the second paragraph of the Contract, in its published form, includes two sentences that are intended to sum up the significance of the new Republican majority in the House of Representatives: "That historic change would be the end of government that is too big, too intrusive, and too easy with the public's money. It can be the beginning of a Congress that respects the values and shares the faith of the American family."

I was very interested, therefore, in turning to "Strengthen Families and Protect Our Kids," the section of the Contract that explicitly deals with the family. What I found is the Family Reinforcement Act, which (again quoting from the published Contract):

(1) protects parents' rights to supervise their children's participation in any federally funded program and shield them from federally sponsored surveys that involve intrusive questioning; (2) requires states to give "full faith and credit" to child support orders issued by the courts or the administrative procedures of other states; (3) provides a refundable tax credit of up to $5,000 for families adopting a child; (4) strengthens penalties for child pornography and criminal conduct involving minors; and (5) provides a $500 tax credit for families caring for a dependent elderly parent.

To which my response can be summed up in two words: "That's it?"

Except for the first provision, about shielding children from "intrusive questioning" in "federally funded surveys," the need for which frankly escapes me, I'm in favor of all this proposed legislation. The problem is that in and of itself, it will do next to nothing to "strengthen families and protect our kids." For one thing, the specific measures tend to be either irrelevant or not forceful enough. Caring for elderly relatives at home is laudable in the extreme, and it should be encouraged. But to what extent will a $500 tax credit—amounting to a savings of not much more than $100 a year for most Americans—actually encourage this? Not much, I would submit. A $5,000 adoption tax credit is more like it, but even the $1,000-plus cash savings it would represent doesn't come close to defraying the amount of money many people spend in the course of adopting a child. So it amounts to moral support for adoptive parents—a worthy but not especially significant endeavor. And while no one could be a more enthusiastic supporter than I in putting some teeth in our system of collecting child-support payments, the Contract's provision has about as much bite as an eighteen-month-old.

Of course, the Contract deals with issues of family in another area: welfare reform. As you no doubt recall, among other things, the Contract specified that, in the interest of bolstering its conception of family values, mothers under the age of eighteen would no longer receive AFDC (Aid to Families with Dependent Children) payments for children born out of wedlock, and that states must drop families from the AFDC program after they have received a total of five years of benefits.

I have my own ideas about the relationship between the welfare system and the American family, and I will share them with you shortly. But what I want to say now is that if you believe government action can have an effect on the state of the family in a nation—as do both I and the Republicans who signed the Contract with America—then the government should *take* action.

I write this when most of the Contract is still in the legislative process, and it is unclear in what form it will emerge. But it is clear that for the time being the Contract has set the legislative agenda, that whatever does emerge will be a variation on it. And that, at least as far as the family goes, is a shame. With the national attention focused on the family, this could have been a perfect time for a broad public discussion on what is the most efficacious, most humane, and most forward-thinking way to approach family policy. That has most assuredly not happened. The Republican platform for the family is, to paraphrase Shakespeare, a lot of sound and fury, signifying not much of anything. In other words, if we're going to have a proactive, truly beneficial family policy, let's have one. Let's not just wave the family banner and then, when push comes to shove, come up with a few mild programs and a lot of empty and often divisive rhetoric.

Over the past half-century or more, government action has come, pure and simple, in the form of dollars: social programs, grants, and other forms of spending. And, in an ideal world, I would have the government generously subsidize every one of the fine profamily programs I discussed in the last chapter. But I know that, given the current political climate, it would make no sense to expect this to happen. Nevertheless, there are far more ways the government can help the American family than are discussed in the Contract with America, and I will discuss some of them over the rest of this chapter.

As I see it, there are seven general areas in which family policy can have a truly significant impact:

1. The welfare system
2. Government regulation of business
3. The schools
4. Taxation
5. Child-support payments
6. The economy
7. A general commitment to the family

In the rest of this chapter I will address all seven of these areas.

WELFARE

I hasten to assure everyone that you are not about to read a detailed disquisition on the American welfare system. It is a complicated, contentious, vexing subject, and far better minds than mine have devoted entire books to it. What I would like to do is spend a little time talking about the relationship between welfare and family—specifically, between welfare and the rise of low-income single-mother households.

Lately, the conventional wisdom (shown most dramatically in the aforementioned Contract with America) has held that the relationship is direct and causal. In other words, the fact that young, single women who have babies become eligible for AFDC *motivates* them to have babies. The corollary, of course, is that if AFDC rules are changed so that payments are not automatic (or, in some cases, even obtainable), behavior will change as a result, and these women will not have out-of-wedlock babies at anything like the present rate.

A spokesman for this point of view is former Education Secretary William Bennett, who testified before Congress last year in favor of cutting off welfare payments for unmarried teenage mothers. "You would actually see fewer children born out of wedlock," he testified. "You would see less misery, and you would break the cycle of poverty."

I think this reasoning is full of holes, and I will tell you why. First of all, it rests on two related basic assumptions that are demonstrably false: first, that welfare payments are a significant motivating factor when it comes to poor single women having babies and, second, that when those payments are reduced or eliminated, there will be a resulting lowering of the out-of-wedlock birthrate.

How do I know these assumptions are false? Consider these facts: Between 1970 and 1993, the out-of-wedlock birthrate jumped some threefold. Yet in the same period, the average welfare benefit per family, adjusted for inflation, went *down* 45 percent, from $676 a month to $374 a month (in 1993 dollars). It would seem absurd to think that this "bonanza" (it amounts to a total of $4,488 a year—less than 40 percent of the official poverty guideline for the typical AFDC family of three) would have any kind of effect on anyone's behavior.

Also bear in mind that while the illegitimacy rate among the poor nearly doubled from 1979 to 1992, it also doubled among those who *weren't* poor and *weren't* getting welfare checks—strongly suggesting that other forces were at work. Indeed, so skewed had the public debate about these issues become that in 1994 a group of prominent social scientists issued a joint statement that "focusing on welfare as the primary cause of out-of-wedlock childbearing vastly oversimplifies this phenomenon."

University of Pennsylvania sociologist Elijah Anderson agrees. "Many people are engaging in so many of these practices [that is, having unprotected sex before marriage] out of a sense of despair, of having no stake in the system," he says. "When people have a stake in the system, they are more careful about behavior that could in some ways undermine it."

In 1993, the state of New Jersey passed a law denying additional welfare payments when mothers already receiving aid had additional children. Previously, a mother would have gotten an extra $102 a month after the birth of a second child, and $64 a month for every child beyond that. Predictably, as of yet it has not had a perceptible effect on the rate of childbearing among these women. One woman who had a fourth child while on the program told the *New York Times,* "It wasn't planned, but I wasn't going to abort her. Sixty-four dollars is not going to change my love for my children, and if I would have aborted her, it wouldn't have comforted my soul."

The woman's reference to abortion brings up what is, to my mind, the supreme hypocrisy of many conservative politicians who favor limiting or eliminating welfare payments. I would rank the likelihood of these kind of policies affecting actual behavior as follows: Increased sexual abstinence? Virtually no effect. Increased use of contraception? Unfortunately, minimal. Increased abortion rates? Yes. For before you actually know you are pregnant everything is in the realm of the theoretical, a realm we all know most teenagers aren't very familiar or comfortable with. The moment is their world, and as for the consequences, well, why worry about them? Sitting in a doctor's office and being told that a baby is on the way, with no expectation of AFDC benefits, might be the one time when a young woman might decide *not* to go ahead and have that child.

Yet many if not most of these politicians are staunch abortion opponents. One possible conclusion is that they don't have the mental capacity to think their proposals through. Another is that they are hypocrites, or worse: In other words, abortion is morally indefensible for people like them, but for the poor, the black, the Hispanic, it's okay.

Another myopic aspect of these proposals is that they almost completely overlook the *fathers* of these children, many of whom are in their twenties or older and literally could not care less about AFDC payments. The welfare-reductions-to-reduce-illegitimacy idea puts the entire burden on the woman, which is not only wrongheaded but unfair.

If these proposals won't cause a significant change in behavior, what will they cause? Robert C. Granger of the Manpower Demonstration Research Corporation, which studies welfare experiments around the country, was recently quoted in the *New York Times* on the idea of cutting off welfare benefits for mothers under eighteen. "The biggest group," he said, "would have the baby and be poorer than they would have been."

And the fact is, the main effect of these proposals would be increased suffering, as even their proponents must recognize. And it would be suffering borne primarily by children. Of the 14 million people on AFDC, about two-thirds—some 9.7 million—are children. If all the welfare provisions in the Contract with America had been passed, more than 5 million of them would have lost their financial support.

The question then arises, What will become of these children? It was in answer to this that Speaker of the House Newt Gingrich made his famous suggestion of orphanages. Now, orphanages are a subject on which I am qualified to speak, having spent my tenth through my sixteenth year in one. I know that they can provide a great deal of good, and also that they can never be a substitute for the love of a mother and father. I think they—or, more generally, some kind of group home—may have a place in the America of today. If a mother cannot afford to live on her own, or cannot (or will not) support her children, then there should be public facilities available, a supportive environment where, on the one hand, she can live with her kids until she can get back on her feet, or, on the other, where children can get attention, care, support, and a good education.

I would imagine that I differ with Mr. Gingrich on the issue of compulsion. I would forcibly remove children from their mother only in the most extreme circumstances, involving neglect or abuse, and never because of her financial condition. Otherwise, I am all for such publicly supported homes. But I wonder if this isn't another bit of disingenuousness. The Republicans present themselves as cost-cutting, government-shrinking budget slashers. Yet consider: The cost of educating and housing each child at Boys Town, a model orphanage if ever there was one, runs between

$40,000 and $48,000 *a year*. If they are slashing school-lunch and summer-job programs, are we really expected to believe that they will be willing to bankroll a nationwide network of labor-intensive and capital-intensive institutions whose cost will undoubtedly run into the billions of dollars?

No, I believe that cutting welfare to the extent that has been proposed would result in a level of suffering that has not been seen in this country since the Great Depression. And even though "welfare reform" has been a battle cry on almost all points on the political spectrum, I do not believe that the American people want this to happen. A recent *New York Times*/CBS News poll asked about "Government spending on welfare." Forty-eight percent of the respondents said it should be cut; 13 percent said it should be increased. But when asked about "spending programs for poor children"—which is pretty much what AFDC is—47 percent called for increases and only 9 percent for cuts.

Let me comment on one more aspect of the welfare debate: the currently popular notion of shifting responsibility for welfare from the federal government to state governments. The idea is to give the states block grants for welfare, as well as broad discretion on how to design and administer their programs. I think this is a colossally *bad* idea. It would lead to slashes in benefits, increased suffering, and, potentially, a kind of 1990s version of the Depression-era Dust Bowl migration, in which poor families wander from state to state trying to find a haven.

All this is not to say that I am in support of the current welfare program. While I do not believe it has been especially harmful in and of itself, I also do not believe that it has been beneficial. Generally, I am in favor of "workfare"—that is, programs that tie welfare benefits to job-training, job-getting, and job-holding.

The conservatives talk a lot about work; their "welfare reforms" tend to remove a mother from the rolls if she isn't gainfully employed within a certain amount of time after giving birth. I think they're talking out of both sides of their mouths. Getting welfare mothers into meaningful jobs in the labor force requires a great deal of training, support, and probably even job creation through public-works programs. All of these things are very expensive (though I believe they more than pay for themselves in the long run), and therefore are an anathema to conservatives. I suppose they would call them "pork."

A truly feasible workfare program also requires a strong commitment to high-quality day care—essentially, making sure it is available and affordable to every working mother. This is equally expensive, and virtually all workfare proposals, including President Clinton's, have tended to skimp on it—a tragic mistake, in my view. But whoever pays for it, working mothers are going to need day care, and this points up yet another bit of conservative doublespeak. It has been the conservatives, has it not, who have been the loudest bemoaners of the return of mothers to the workforce, in large part because of the dire consequences of separating young children from their moms? Yet here they are recommending—indeed, *insisting*—that welfare moms go to work. Once again, the implication is clear: It's not okay for us, but it's okay for them.

The truth is, it's okay for everybody, but poor, single women, far more than anyone else, need *support*. After all, many middle-class moms have cars, microwaves, husbands, and all the other conveniences that make child-rearing a little easier; they also have the money to go out to McDonald's once in a while. Unless we make sure that support systems are in place, and that good-quality day care is available and affordable, it is both heartless and foolish to force mothers on welfare to enter the workforce.

REGULATION

On February 5, 1993, President Clinton signed into law the Family and Medical Leave Act, a bill specifying that companies employing more than fifty workers must grant employees up to twelve weeks of unpaid leave annually to care for a new child or a seriously ill family member, or to recover from an illness. Unfortunately, it didn't cover enough people (only about 44 percent of women and 50 percent of men in the workforce).

And, once you read the small print, it didn't seem all that impressive. (As noted earlier, most European countries mandate *paid* leave, of a significantly longer duration.)

But it was long overdue, and it was a start. It was, in addition, an example of the kind of proactive, profamily legislation it's possible for our government to pass. I am very well aware that the current mood is antiregulation. But all things pass, and I am sure this eventually will, too.

When it does, one of the first things I want our lawmakers to take a look at is the day-care industry. A recent nationwide study by researchers at four universities highlighted the poor care that is all too prevalent, especially in the case of infants and toddlers. The study found that up to 40 percent of these youngest children received "poor" care. Overall, only one in seven of the centers studied offered the kind of warm relationships and intellectual stimulation that are necessary for healthy emotional and psychological development.

It would be all too easy to draw the wrong conclusion from these findings. As Jay Belsky, a professor of human development at Pennsylvania State University, was quoted as saying in the *New York Times,* "The mistake would be concluding that only parents can care for young children and that day care is inherently problematical. When high-quality, stable care is provided, there is good evidence that children thrive."

And when is high-quality, stable care provided? By and large, when the money is there to pay for it. The national study found that the centers providing high-quality care spent roughly 10 percent more per child than those providing mediocre care. When parents can afford to pay and are willing to spend those extra dollars, everything is fine. But often that is not the case, which is why, even if it doesn't make direct grants to any other family-related enterprises or programs, the government truly needs to subsidize day care.

Short of that, it needs to regulate. In 1992, the state of Florida passed legislation tightening staffing requirements at day-care centers. For example, where previously it was acceptable to have one adult for every six babies under a year old, the new law set a limit of four babies for each adult. The Families and Work Institute, a nonprofit research group in New York, studied conditions in 150 licensed centers in the state both before and after the law. It found that under the new standards, children engaged in more complex play, had better language skills, and had fewer behavioral problems. Not surprisingly, the *teachers* behaved better, too, being much less likely to respond to misbehavior with "negative management styles" like yelling, threatening, or hitting.

So let's take a cue from Florida and give all our children a break.

Another industry that could be regulated to positive results for the American family is television. The Children's Television Act of 1990 declared that in order to have their FCC licenses renewed, television stations must serve the "educational and informational needs of children." It has had a generally beneficial effect: After the Act took effect, such excellent programs as *Bill Nye, the Science Guy; Cro; Beakman's World;* and *Where in the World Is Carmen Sandiego?* came on the air. And the amount of "educational and informational" programming on the average station went up from a very modest two hours a week to a slightly less modest three and a half hours a week.

The trouble was, the Act didn't define what "educational and informational" meant, so you had the spectacle of stations citing such programs as *G.I. Joe* and *The Jetsons* as fulfilling their obligations. And the truth is, these concepts *are* hard to define.

The solution, it seems to me, lies in the fact that we already have a network providing absolutely wonderful children's programming that is educational and informative by *anyone's* definition: PBS. (That, of course, is in addition to such cable services as the Disney Channel, the Family Network, and Nickelodeon. Unfortunately, not every family can afford cable.) Once again, I know Washington is in a cost-cutting mood. But at the very least we should keep a watchful eye on *Sesame Street, Barney, The*

Magic School Bus, Lamb Chop, and all the rest. If corporate underwriting, licensing fees, and public donations can balance their budgets, wonderful. But to the extent they can't, there would be no better service for the government to provide than to chip in the rest.

SCHOOLS

There is no more dramatic interface between the government and the family than the public schools. Second only to the home, school is where children learn to interact with others, learn citizenship, learn values. It is where they spend their time.

Which makes it all the more important that schools be designed and operated under a philosophy that recognizes the importance of family. Not long ago, I asked Secretary of Education Richard Riley for his thoughts on how they might accomplish this, and I'd like to share his answer with you:

> There are concrete steps that schools can take to reinforce the parental role in helping their children learn:
>
> *Overcome the jargon gap.* While teachers like to share their specialized knowledge with concerned parents, parents can experience basic communications problems with the school because of their inability to understand the professional jargon used by school staff. Schools should make every effort to communicate with parents in a straightforward and simple fashion. Some school-parent newsletters have actually begun including a glossary of terms for parents to better understand school improvement efforts.
>
> *Reduce mistrust and cultural barriers.* Schools can address issues of misperception, distrust, and different cultural styles on the part of both families and teachers by making contacts

nonthreatening in neutral settings. These activities might include resource centers, informal learning sessions, home visits by parent liaisons, and meetings off school grounds. Because such problems can run deep, however, more comprehensive approaches are often needed.

Address language barriers. Schools should make accommodations to reach parents whose first language is not English. While translating materials into their native language can be useful for these parents, schools should not rely on written communications alone. Ideally, schools should have a resource person available who can communicate with parents in their native language either through face-to-face meetings or via the telephone. Low-level technologies, like interactive telephone voice mail systems that have bilingual recordings for parents, are also very useful.

Conduct a parent survey. Another step that schools can take to bridge the distance between families and schools is to conduct a parent survey to find out concerns and opinions of parents about the school in general. The Linda Vista School in San Diego, California, conducted an extensive parent survey when beginning a comprehensive process to improve the school. To make sure all parents were reached, the school translated the survey into Spanish, Vietnamese, and Hmong, in addition to English. Including families from the beginning of the reform process helped establish a sense of shared responsibility for school improvement. From this survey evolved a school reform process that includes all members of the school community, including parents.

Expand opportunities for contact. Many schools hold evening and weekend meetings and conferences before school to accommodate parents' work schedules. By remaining open in the afternoons, in the evenings and on weekends, schools can promote various recreational and learning activities including adult education and training in parenting, and can create a safe haven against neighborhood crime. The National Education Commission on Time and Learning recently recommended extended day and year programs to help American students learn more. The Murfreesboro schools in Tennessee are now open from 6:00 A.M. to 6:00 P.M, and there are plans to open a K–8 year-round school. This schedule grew out of a concern by parents and educators about the number of latchkey children in the community. Over 50 percent of the city's 5,000 elementary school students can be found in the program on any given day. Free transportation and child care can also assist parents in low-income and unsafe neighborhoods. Hiring a parent liaison or home-school coordinator is another strategy to develop programs without adding to the tasks of teachers.

Give parents a voice in school decisions. A part of the family involvement goal explicitly states, "Parents and families will help to ensure that schools are adequately supported and will hold schools and teachers to high standards of accountability." Many parents may be reluctant to get involved to this extent, especially those with language differences or mistrust of the schools. But this should be an important component of efforts to involve families more, and schools can do this in many ways. A number of school systems have established new governance arrangements in recent years, including Chicago, where each school has an independent council with strong parent participation, and entire states, such as California and South Carolina, which require school councils with parent representation.

Use new technology. Schools are using a number of new technologies to communicate with parents and students after school hours. One rapidly spreading arrangement is a district-wide homework hotline to help guide students with assignments. The United Federation of Teachers in New York City has operated a homework hotline for more than 12 years. In addition, voice mail systems have been installed in several hundred schools across the country. Parents and students can call for taped messages from teachers describing classroom activities and daily homework assignments.

TAXATION

Our country has a long tradition of using tax policy to further what we collectively see as the social good. We want to encourage people to buy their own homes and to give to charity, and we don't want to *penalize* them for getting sick. As a result, mortgage interest payments, charitable donations, and medical expenses are all tax deductible.

This applies to the family as well. In recognition of the importance of children, and of the expenses they entail, families are entitled to a $2,500 tax exemption per child. This is almost universally considered to be a good idea; the only question is, Should it be increased or otherwise bolstered? The trouble with increasing the tax exemption, as many have pointed out, is that the whole notion of tax breaks favors people with higher incomes. Poor families, whether the parents are employed or not, pay little or no taxes, so a tax exemption will do them no good, and in fact will only serve to widen the gap between them and everyone else.

There is another kind of favoritism inherent in the idea of a tax exemption. In the words of the Communitarian Network's "Position Paper on the Family," "Parents whose income declined because they decided that one of them would stay home while the children are young, parents who share one job, or work less overtime, or are less career-committed because they are especially dedicated to their children—are disadvantaged by such changes in tax law."

So as not to tacitly punish this group, the communitarians recommend, instead of an exemption, a child *allowance*. They suggest an annual figure of $600 per child. It sounds good to me.

One area in which tax policy has inadvertently served a social agenda is the marriage tax. If you are in a two-paycheck marriage, you know exactly what I am talking about. If not, I'll briefly explain. Until 1969, the tax code was such that a married couple where only one spouse was working was permitted, for tax purposes, to split the working spouse's income between them, thus lowering the total tax owed. Quite understandably, this was viewed as an unfair disadvantage for single workers, who could not split their incomes with anybody. And so Congress ruled that couples had to pool their incomes (whether one or both spouses were working) and pay taxes based on the total amount.

Sounds good, but it has turned out to be a rather stiff penalty on married couples who work. (It was stiffened further in 1993, when the marginal tax rate rose from 31 to 36 percent on married couples with taxable incomes of $140,000 or more—but not on single filers until their incomes reached $115,000.) Consider these examples. A working couple, each of whom makes $27,550, would face a tax liability of $10,488. But if they were not married, they would only have to pay $9,514, a difference of $974. As income goes up, so does the penalty, maxing out for couples who earn $500,000. A husband and wife who each earn $250,000 would pay a total of $174,305 in taxes—a whopping $15,025 more than if they hadn't tied the knot.

This is patently unfair. Worse than that, it sends absolutely the wrong message regarding our society's commitment to marriage. An obvious way to correct it would be to allow a working husband and wife to file separately. A more gradual shift would be to provide a tax deduction on a certain part of the lower wage earner's income. Whatever the approach, something's got to be done.

Some extremely creative things can be done with tax policy. Futurist David Pearce Snyder has suggested allowing large extended families to incorporate themselves as businesses. And why not? It doesn't make sense that families should be denied the kind of tax breaks long granted to corporations. For example, there could be write-offs for money spent helping the family as a whole, and exemptions for wealth transferred within the family.

But what should not be lost sight of, as I suggested earlier, is that tax policy only has a noticeable effect on Americans who are middle class or wealthier. It doesn't do much for our poor children and families, who are in the most dire straits.

CHILD SUPPORT

Absent fathers—"deadbeat dads"—who do not pay court-ordered child-support payments have long been recognized as a significant problem. Unfortunately, for an equally long time there has been resistance to doing something about them on the part of the middle-class and upper-middle-class males who, by and large, run our government. Mary Jo Bane, who before becoming assistant secretary for children and families in the U.S. Health and Human Services Department was social services commissioner in New York state, gave me an insight into this when we talked in her Washington office. "In New York, when we were instituting child-support laws, all these members of the legislature made high-minded statements about 'privacy,' " she says. "At the same time, you could tell that they were secretly calculating how much *they* would owe."

Fortunately, New York passed its law, and steps have been taken nationally as well. The Family Support Act of 1988 required states to increase efforts to establish paternity at birth, to develop standards for setting and updating awards, and to create mechanisms for withholding child-support obligations from earnings.

Unfortunately, compliance has been lax, and at present there is a shortfall of more than $30 billion between what is supposed to be paid and what is paid.

There are a number of ways more teeth could be put into collection of child support. The Communitarian Network's "Position

Paper on the Family" advocates using the Internal Revenue Service to dock wages of deadbeats, and proposes requiring states to attempt to establish paternity at the time of birth, then include both parents on a child's birth certificate. Some have gone farther, suggesting denying driver's licenses and other privileges, and perhaps even jailing fathers who don't pay court-ordered support.

Recognizing that many absent fathers simply don't have the money to pay, theorist Sara McClanahan favors the carrot approach, proposing that the nonresident parent be guaranteed a minimum-wage job. I like this notion. Trying to extract payments from unemployed fathers is, in the words of a phrase used by many welfare mothers, like trying to get "blood from a turnip."

One of the most aggressive states in this area has been Georgia, which began to step up its collection effort in 1989. That year, $36 million in child support payments was collected; in 1993, $85 million was collected. The state has taken some truly innovative steps, including sending state workers to the maternity wards of hospitals carrying affidavits of paternity. The thinking is that the period after a child's birth, when warm, fuzzy feelings are all around, is the best time to get a father to step forward. That information may prove useful later, if he becomes less vocal about his identity.

But even in Georgia the results have not been earth-shattering. The average payment is about $100 a month, not nearly enough to remove most recipients from the welfare rolls.

And, in fact, while the spectacle of deadbeat dads is morally offensive, the truth is that it doesn't make a huge difference in the lives of women and children receiving welfare. Professor Irwin Garfinkel, an authority on child support at Columbia University, was recently quoted in the *New York Times* as saying, "If you think it's going to get rid of welfare, that's ignorant. If we had a perfect system and collected 100 percent of child support, we would still only cut welfare by 25 percent."

No, child-support collection is not a panacea. But there is one way that the government can truly help poor and struggling families, and that is . . .

THE ECONOMY

Of all the things that government can do to help the American family, the most significant have to do with jobs. If our people don't have the opportunity for decent-paying work, the consequences for the family are dire. After all, who can concentrate on "family values" when there is no food on the table?

"Trying to build a strong economy where a family can have jobs is the first thing," Carol Rasko, President Clinton's senior adviser for domestic affairs, told me. "If you can do that, then you can address health care, and then you can address all the other things."

I don't believe it is the responsibility of the government to furnish every citizen with a job. Yet it is the government's function to ensure that the economy is functioning properly. And our economy has some serious problems, at least insofar as our people are concerned. In the last few generations, we have witnessed a dramatic shift from an *industrial* to a service-oriented economy. That might be fine in terms of our ability to compete in the global marketplace, and it may be wonderful for your average cable-television executive, but it has had dire consequences for many of our people. As factories have moved out of the cities (to rural areas in some cases, to foreign countries in others) they have taken with them millions of relatively high-wage jobs. What opportunities are left for unskilled individuals? The most menial service jobs (that is, flipping hamburgers at McDonald's), welfare, street hustling, or out-and-out criminal activities.

The situation is obviously not good for the people of the inner cities and their families. It leads to hopelessness, illegitimacy, all kinds of pathologies (like crime, substance and domestic abuse, mental illness), and, in general, a ripping apart of the social fabric.

What can government do about it? Two areas of action come to mind. The first consists of packages of low taxes and outright grants—"enterprise zones," as they are often called—that will encourage businesses to return to the cities. The free market, as an idea, is fine, but if left completely free it will ultimately lead to the death of our cities. Sometimes the pump simply has to be primed, and this is one of those times.

The second and even more important area is education. Information and service jobs are the wave of the future, and, unlike factory jobs, they *demand* highly trained workers. We must make a dramatic, unprecedented investment in our young people so that they will be equipped to function and, eventually, thrive in this world. I'm talking about *billions* of dollars poured into new schools, into improvements in our existing schools, into computers and teachers' salaries and physical plants. I'm talking about a complete rethinking of the way we go about educating kids.

In this regard, we should be following the lead of Walter Annenberg, the former owner of *TV Guide* and ambassador to the United Kingdom, who in recent years has donated hundreds of millions of dollars to schools, many of them in our cities. He has the right idea. We as a people need to follow through on his groundbreaking work, by donating money (on a lesser level), by volunteering our time, and by *paying attention*.

COMMITMENT

All of the things I've been talking about are very practical, a diverse group of actions involving spending money and changing laws. But the importance of symbolism should not be forgotten. Perhaps as much as specific programs, it is critical that the government be *seen* as having a commitment to the family.

"One of the main things that has struck me in this job is the importance of the signaling function of public policies," says Assistant Secretary of Health and Human Services Mary Jo Bane. "They symbolize a set of values and aspirations, and they're just as important as the particular things you do. Tough provisions about child support, for example, is a statement that both parents are responsible. Even if they never deter a single young man from getting a girl pregnant, it's a very important statement about public policy. People see it on the news, on talk shows, in the newspapers, and they start to think, 'This is something I need to take seriously.' "

There are also government actions that, in and of themselves, will not have a particularly broad effect, but that will send a powerful message about the family. I'm thinking, for example, of laws relating to adoption. Everyone agrees that adoption is a very good thing: It places many otherwise unwanted children in loving homes, it is an alternative to abortion, and, in general, it strengthens the family. Yet many people who want to adopt and who would make wonderful parents often have a very difficult time doing so; for instance gay couples and individuals of one race who want to adopt a child of another race. I am enthusiastically in favor of changing our adoption laws and procedures so that these circumstances are considered as irrelevant as they are and only the truly important questions are considered: Will the prospective parent or parents love the child? Will they have the resources to care for him or her?

For an analogy to the kind of broad-based commitment I'm talking about, think of the environmental movement that began some twenty-five years ago. It wasn't just a series of legislative acts; it was a concerted *campaign,* in which every effort related to the common goal. Laws were passed, to be sure, but consciousnesses were also raised.

One thing the family movement might borrow from the "tree huggers" is the notion of the environmental impact statement. Whenever a project of a certain size is contemplated the engineers must draft a statement assessing the effect the project will have on the environment, its approval depending in part on what the statement says. How about requiring that every piece of legislation, and every major action by a regulated business, carry with it a *family* impact statement—an explanation, endorsed by experts, of its probable effect on families and children? This may have little or no practical value, but the symbolism would be enormous.

The same goes for another idea I have long favored, the creation of a new cabinet-level post devoted to the family. This would be filled by a universally respected authority who would oversee the progress of family-oriented legislation, monitor all those impact statements, and deliver an annual "state of the American family" message. As to the title this official would have, that is a no-brainer. Remember during the energy crisis when we had an "oil czar"? The family crisis is just as pressing, so by all means let's have a *family* czar.

CHAPTER VIII

What American Business Can Do for the Family

The first thing you notice is a security guard sitting in front of a bank of video monitors. He greets the kids and their parents with a smile and a wave as he buzzes them in; in the event that an unfamiliar adult comes to pick up a child, he will phone the boy or girl's parent and get their approval.

It's not the way things usually are done in day-care centers. Nor is this one located in an area where security is a particular concern: The Great Expectations learning center is on site at MBNA America's corporate headquarters in a quiet office park in suburban Oglestown, Delaware, a nonthreatening locale if ever there was one. But, as any parent who has ever had a child in day care can tell you, the more security, the better. Even in the seemingly safest environment, anything can happen: a divorced parent intent on abduction, a robber who doesn't realize that he's about to stick up a day-care center, or other possibilities too terrible even to think about. But there usually *isn't* security, simply because the child-care industry has traditionally been run on the proverbial shoestring. So in the rare case when things are done as they really should be, it's a shock.

As you're buzzed inside by the guard (after confirming that you really have reason to be there), you can see that at Great Expectations, one of four on-site centers for employees of MBNA, a 7,000-

174

employee bank specializing in "affinity" credit cards, just about everything is done as it should be. Whereas too many child-care centers are stuck in dark basements or big warehouse-like rooms, Great Expectations is in its own custom-designed building; it's light, airy, brightly colored, and divided into classrooms and common areas that aren't too big and aren't too small but are just right. The walls are filled with children's artwork. And whereas most centers are isolated from parents, here there's a constant stream of moms and dads dropping off their kids, picking them up, just stopping by to spend time with them or have lunch with them or, in some cases, to *be* lunch (there's a special area for nursing mothers).

Perhaps the most striking difference, explains Maureen Byrnes, MBNA's "People Advocate" and a guide at Great Expectations, concerns staff training and compensation, the scandalously low level of which is a national disgrace. "Our director has a Ph.D. from the University of Delaware," she says. "Teachers have to have a four-year degree in early childhood development or a related field. They make $24,000 a year, plus benefits and incentives." Despite the high overhead and salary expenses, MBNA is committed to charging a tuition that is at or below the average in the area—depending on the age of the child, between $65 and $103 per week. The resulting deficit is bankrolled by the company; Byrnes won't say how much it amounts to, but it can't be small change.

All this being the case, it's not surprising that although MBNA has three separate child-care centers in Oglestown and its other headquarters, in Camden, Maine, serving about 600 children, there is an eighteen-month waiting list for babies. (As I write this, there is a third office nearing completion, in Wilmington, Delaware, with two more child-care centers on the drawing board. When they are completed, MBNA will have more on-site child care than any corporation in America.) That being the case, it's important that prospective users sign up as quickly as possible—that is, before the baby is born. "We always say, 'Call us the next morning, not that night,' " Byrnes says with a chuckle. (For those on the list, the company provides referrals to and place-ment in other area programs.)

On-site child care is only the most visible of MBNA's profamily programs. Some of the others include:

• **Family leave.** Mothers are eligible for six weeks of paid disabil-ity leave (eight weeks in the case of cesarean section), plus an addi-tional week of paid leave, after the birth of a child. Fathers are eligible for one week of paid leave. And mothers or fathers can take unlimited unpaid leave after a child's birth, with the guarantee of a job in their division upon their return.

• **Adoption assistance.** Workers are eligible for reimbursement of up to $5,000 in expenses and for up to four weeks of paid leave after the adoption of a child.

• **Gradual return policy.** Since many new mothers find it diffi-cult to return immediately to a full-time schedule, MBNA offers them the option of working anywhere from twenty to the full forty hours a week after their return. In a corporate setting, full-time managers are often expected to work a good deal more than forty hours a week, which can wreak havoc on a new family. In a highly innovative program, MBNA offers them the option of working a twenty-five- to thirty-five-hour week, for up to two years, with no expectation of additional hours.

• **Sick days.** Employees are permitted to use up to three sick days a year for the illness of a child. (In addition, the on-site day-care centers have registered nurses on the premises, and special areas where ill children can be cared for.)

• **Marriage benefits.** Employees getting married are given $500, a week's pay, plus the use of one of the company's fleet of antique cars and limousines for their wedding.

Then there are the unclassifiable profamily policies, like free short-term emotional or substance-abuse counseling for employees and their family members and free financial counseling. One re-markable program offers $4,000 a year toward tuition payments to any employee with a child or children in college. (Students with a

3.0 grade point average or better are eligible for a $10,000-a-year scholarship.) I think my favorite feature of the company is the cafeteria, which Byrnes's husband refers to as "the best restaurant in Delaware." It's also a profamily resource. The management encourages employees to order its low-cost, high-quality dinners to be wrapped up and taken home, thus going some distance toward solving the age-old it's-six-o'clock-and-I-just-got-home-and-there's-nothing-to-feed-the-kids dilemma. Also in the cafeteria is a phone booth that employees may use to make free calls to anywhere "within a reasonable area."

MBNA says it believes in supporting the family, and I'm sure that is true. But it wouldn't do all these things if it didn't think they helped the bottom line. And in that regard the evidence is clear. In the banking industry, the costs involved in recruiting, interviewing, training, and retaining employees is among the biggest items on the balance sheet. And it seems unquestionable that MBNA's family policies have helped it keep these costs way, way down. Some 80 percent of its employees are "referrals"—that is, people who come to the company because friends or relatives recommend it to them. And where the industry averages an employee turnover rate of some 20 percent a year, at MBNA that figure is an astonishingly low *6 percent*. And all this is over and above the increased productivity that can be expected of workers who can clear their minds of domestic worries as much as possible.

What's happened at MBNA is really not surprising. A host of studies (in addition to plain old intuition) have demonstrated that when companies pay attention to family needs, everybody benefits: workers, their supervisors, and, yes, the bottom line. At AT&T, it was calculated that the average cost of giving new parents a year of unpaid leave was 32 percent of the worker's annual salary, while to permanently replace that worker would cost 150 percent. In addition, 88 percent of surveyed AT&T employees reported that the profamily programs caused them to feel a greater sense of loyalty to the company. This finding was borne out in a study of the Fel-Pro Corporation by University of Chicago researchers: Employees who had used work-family programs had the highest performance evaluations and loyalty to the company. Overall, according to a 1994 study by Work/Family Directions, a consulting firm, for every dollar a company spends on flexible work or family benefits, there is a return of two to six dollars through reduced absenteeisms, increased motivation, and higher rates of retention.

Such issues are more important than ever now, for at least two reasons. First, as I have discussed many times in this book, the day of the stay-at-home mom is pretty much over, for good or ill. More often than not, both a child's parents work, and employers simply have to understand this when thinking through their expectations and obligations regarding their employees. (Of course, the pressure is even greater in a single-parent family when the parent works.) Second, because of downsizing and the tightening of the economy in general, the typical American worker works more hours than ever before. Again, the effect on the family is stressful, and, again, companies have an obligation to do what they can to ease the pressure.

For some time now, the more forward-thinking American corporations have understood these truths; some of them have gone beyond the call of duty and started to lead the way to what I hope will be a paradigm shift in the way business looks at the family. Every year *Working Mother* magazine publishes a list of the "100 Best Companies for Working Mothers." (Since in our culture, mothers are assigned the bulk of responsibilities regarding family, this translates into the "100 Best Companies for *Families*.") If only to give the best of the best a little more time in the spotlight, let me tip my hat to *Working Mother*'s top ten (in alphabetical order). All have generous leave policies and dependent-care assistance, so I'll highlight some of their more distinctive programs.

AT&T. In 1990, AT&T—together with two unions that service its employees—launched a Family Care Development Fund, which each year distributes several million dollars toward developing family-oriented programs.

Barnett Bank. This Florida bank has made a major commitment to supporting child care (no doubt tied to the fact that women are chief executives of four units and make up 44 percent of the company's highest paid employees). The company offers four on-site child-care centers, direct subsidies for employees using other centers, and will even reimburse child-care costs for nonroutine business travel.

Fel-Pro. This is a Chicago-area manufacturer that is constantly seeking to improve its work-family programs. Most recently, Fel-Pro increased its financial aid for adoption from $2,500 to $5,000 and its tuition-refund benefit up to a maximum of $6,500.

Glaxo. Other companies have on-site day-care centers, but few subsidize them as heavily as this North Carolina drug manufacturer. Depending on their income, employees can pay as little as $30 a week for high-quality care.

IBM. The computer giant has the most generous family leave of any American company—up to three years, some of it at full pay. Equally important, employees apparently feel that taking advantage of the leave doesn't hurt their career prospects and are therefore not reluctant to do so. In 1993, nearly 1,700 took the leave, staying out for an average of a year and a half.

John Hancock. At John Hancock, employees can take up to a full year of family leave—not only for the birth (or adoption) of a child, but also for care of elderly parents. The leave is unpaid, but they retain all benefits, and if they return within six months, their old job is guaranteed.

Johnson & Johnson. J&J, which supports four on-site child-care centers, has found that absenteeism is 50 percent lower among users of its family programs than among its employees as a whole.

Lancaster Laboratories. This Pennsylvania company has just one on-site center—but considering that there are only 500 employees compared to J&J's 30,000-plus, that's pretty good. Lancaster credits its work-family programs with keeping annual turnover at 8 percent, one-third the industry average.

NationsBank. Often left behind in work-family programs are employees at the low end of the salary scale. At NationsBank, employees with family incomes of $35,000 or less are eligible for subsidies that cover up to 50 percent of child-care costs.

Xerox. One thing about Xerox that should *definitely* be copied is its "LifeCycle Assistance" program, which was introduced in 1993 and is designed to assist employees in balancing work and family demands by providing money for expenses not covered in the traditional benefits plan. The plan subsidizes child-care costs, pays first-time house buyers up to $2,000 toward a down payment or closing costs, and provides employees funds for purchase of health insurance for otherwise uncovered household members, including siblings, parents, grandparents, and—most notably—same- or opposite-sex domestic partners.

As I say, I applaud these and other companies that have instituted programs that attempt to help workers solve the job-family challenge. But it would be a mistake to place all the emphasis on programs per se.

To illustrate what I mean, let me get personal for a moment and ask you to consider *my* job. I work very hard: seeing clients, giving talks and lectures all over the country, writing articles and books like this one. But for all the hours I put in, my work is also characterized by a very high degree of *flexibility*. If I feel things have been too hectic lately, I can decide not to schedule any appearances for a few weeks. If I have an intense, irresistible desire to see my grandson, Ari, I can shuffle my appointments, or block out some writing time on another day. Of course I honor my commitments, but the point is that if I need time for my family or myself, I can almost always make it. That's what I mean by flexibility. Where corporate programs often have to do with money (providing reimbursement for child care, for example), what many workers really need is *time*.

I realize that I have an unusual situation, to put it mildly—how many *other* four-foot-seven-inch German-born sex therapists are there?—but at the same time, it is undeniable that many, many more people could experience some of the flexibility I enjoy. When you say "job" in America today, the idea that comes to mind is someone sitting at a desk or in a factory from nine to five, every day. Sometimes that's unavoidable, but in many cases it's not. As the year 2000 approaches, American companies will simply have to become receptive to the need to offer their workers more flexibility.

Some of the ways this can be accomplished are obvious—and, to some extent, already in evidence. Flex time is one example. Consider the case of a working couple with school-age children, and how much easier their lives would be if one spouse worked, say, ten to six, and thus would be able to get the kids off to school, while the other worked seven to three and would be at the door for their return? Many working parents would prefer to work part time rather than full time, and would do so if they had the opportunity. Business should be much more forward thinking in structuring some positions to a less-than-forty-hour week.

Certain positions, of course, do not lend themselves to part-time work. In those cases, why not encourage or at least permit job *sharing*? There are already a small but growing number of pioneers who have found a way to work part time in career paths that traditionally demand forty-hour weeks. Their employers, besides being on the cutting edge, reap the benefits of the old adage "Two heads are better than one."

Another way to help ease the job-family crunch is to work at home (commuting time is certainly cut down). People have done so for years, but generally only in certain kinds of jobs: piece workers in the garment industry, writers and artists, some doctors, home day-care workers, and, of course, the original at-home workers, farmers. All told, some 43 million Americans work at home: 30 percent are primarily self-employed, 29 percent are self-employed part time, 21 percent are corporate employees working after hours, and 20 percent are telecommuters.

That last group (translating into more than 9 million people) is the intriguing one. They are people who, by means of technology, are able to carry out their work without opening their front door. The exciting thing is that technology is rapidly advancing, meaning that the possibilities for telecommuting will be, too. For example, the development of new, digital high-speed telephone lines means that people in their home offices are now starting to be able to see each other and transfer massive amounts of data some ten times more quickly than today's high-speed modems do. Before long, there won't be *anything* that many workers won't be able to do at home, except maybe pour each other a cup of coffee. (I'm not downplaying the value of water-cooler communication, but it's a sacrifice that many people would gladly make in favor of the family benefits that telecommuting can provide.)

Once again, some companies have shown themselves to be particularly receptive on flexibility issues. While we're talking about telecommuting, I should point out that at IBM, more than 20,000 people now do all or part of their regular work from home. Pretty much all you need to be a travel agent is a phone, a computer, and a lot of colorful brochures, so it makes sense that American Express travel agents in nine different cities do some work out of their homes.

At First Tennessee National, a bank in Memphis, a group of seven employees responsible for producing 1,400 business customers' statements each month proposed working eleven-hour days earlier in the month, when the statements were issued, in exchange for some personal and family time off later in the month. The company agreed. The result: The time needed to produce the statements went from eight days to five, and seven employees were made very happy.

After employees made it clear that they wanted more time with their families, Corning now offers the option of working four ten-hour days. And at the UNUM Life Insurance Company, more than 150 workers put in an extra hour for nine days and take the tenth day off. One of the most innovative programs is at Miami's Baptist Hospital, where nurses have the option of taking an unpaid leave starting in June and returning to work in September, so as to spend summers with their kids.

Aetna Life & Casualty Co., in Hartford, Connecticut, has proved that when hard times strike, a commitment to employee flexibility doesn't necessarily have to be a victim. The staff has been cut by 24 percent (to 42,000) since 1989, but the number of employees on flex time has risen to nearly 60 percent, part-timers are up 69 percent, and compressed work schedules have doubled.

Several years ago, executives at Deloitte & Touche, an accounting firm based in Wilton, Connecticut, began noticing an alarmingly high turnover rate among women in the managerial ranks.

The company interviewed some 200 women who had recently resigned and found, to management's shock, that about 90 percent *were* working—somewhere else. Their perception tended to be either that the company was inhospitable to women's advancement or that a career at the firm was incompatible with family life.

The company took action, instituting an "Initiative for the Advancement of Women" that seeks to boost women's progress through the firm, assure employees that they will not be penalized for having family concerns, make flexible or part-time schedules widely available, and even counsel employees who seem to be at-risk workaholics that 100-hour weeks aren't a prerequisite for advancement. And Deloitte puts its money where its mouth is: In 1994 a part-time worker named Elizabeth Rader was actually named a partner in the firm—something that would have been unthinkable a few years ago.

The federal government—America's largest employer, with more than 2 million workers—has been perhaps the most outstanding proponent of this type of program, recently mandating a "family-friendly workplace" for every branch of government. The Office of Personnel Management (OPM) promotes options that include working at home, working at conveniently located "telecommuting centers," part-time hours, job sharing, and flexible hours. As of 1994, 52 percent of federal employees were taking advantage of some type of flexible work schedule.

So flexibility is a key. But there's something even more important: attitude. A company can have the longest childbirth leave imaginable and offer telecommuting from here to Timbuktu, but if the corporate culture does not demonstrate an understanding of work-family issues, the results can be disastrous—for both work and family. A study of Merck and Company (one of the leaders in job-family programs) by the Family and Work Institute, a leading think tank, showed that workers in demanding jobs with little support from their supervisors for managing their work and family responsibilities reported that they frequently came home in a "bad mood" and with little energy for their families. And, the study found, people in such situations experienced statistically more tension in their marriages.

On the other hand, the institute concluded in its *National Study of the Changing Workforce*, "Employees with more autonomy in their jobs and more social support from supervisors, co-workers and the workplace culture are more successful in balancing work with family and personal life, experience less work-family conflict and negative job-to-home spillover, are less stressed, and are coping more effectively than other workers."

In sum: "Supervisory support and a family-friendly culture have a greater impact on the employees' family life and the company's bottom line than does the mere use of work-family programs."

But exactly how does a company institute a "family-friendly culture"? It's not entirely clear. A written policy that makes these values clear would help, as would training sessions for all supervisory personnel. Perhaps most important of all are *demonstrations* of the company's commitment, in word and deed, by the top executives.

In this regard, I can't help thinking of a story told to me about President Clinton (who is, after all, the chief executive officer in one particular enterprise, where long hours are part of the corporate culture) when I interviewed Carol Rasko, his senior adviser for domestic affairs:

"One day I was supposed to take Mary Margaret [her teenaged daughter] to a dance recital at six-thirty in the evening," she said. "As I was leaving, people started to look at me in horror. I could tell they were thinking, 'I can't believe she's leaving at five-thirty!' As I headed out the door, I saw the President. Everybody froze. He said, 'Where are you headed?' I told him. He said, 'That's terrific. I think I'll go visiting with Chelsea.'

"Everybody's mouths dropped open."

Don't let the foregoing give you the impression that everything is hunky-dory on the job-family front. Yes, some companies are in the vanguard, and are truly committed to dealing sensitively and progressively with these issues. But they are still decidedly in the minority. And with the economy tightening up, even they are pressured to reverse the gains that were so hard to come by.

I recently spoke to an individual whose job it is to monitor the ways in which American business deals with family issues. And the prognosis I got was far from rosy. "The growth in these programs has been very, very slow," said this person, who asked to remain anonymous. "With the layoff binge and with cost-cutting a priority everywhere, they've been put on the back burner.

"There's no doubt that there have been some very real changes, but the countertrends—overtime and increased workload, job pressure in general—have been much more important. Let's face it, the fundamental culture of American business is work first, families second, and I don't see that changing anytime soon.

"A handful of employers—Motorola, Corning, Aetna—have really managed to cultivate profamily values. But they're up against it. With their competitors—domestically and internationally—squeezing every last drop of productivity out of their workers, these companies are in a bind. They're trying to be good citizens, but their main job, after all, is to create economic value. So what are they going to do?

"You hear a lot about telecommuting. I'm sure it'll grow, and I'm sure that a lot of companies that do it will wave the profamily banner. But let's not kid ourselves. The real reason companies do it isn't because of family values but because of the Clean Air Act and lower costs. When somebody works at home, that's one less office you have to heat, a few hundred less square feet you have to pay rent on. It's debatable whether telecommuting helps the family at all. The notion that because you're physically there, you're helping the family just isn't true. If you're working, you're *working*, and that's not quality time no matter how it's defined."

The figures bear out this bleak analysis. A 1992 survey by the Employee Benefit Research Institute of working mothers with children under thirteen reported the following: 11 percent of their employers offered on-site child care, 9 percent offered dependent-care assistance plans, 8 percent offered child-care resource and referral, 29 percent offered flex time, and 13 percent offered a work-at-home option.

Even in a company that's justly lauded for its commitment to families there can be problems. A study of Johnson & Johnson employees who had used time and leave policies found that 32 percent of them thought they had paid a career price for doing so. Nationally, the returning wage for women who interrupt their careers for family reasons is 33 percent lower than it otherwise would have been; most never make up the gap. Over the course of a lifetime, according to a Rand Corporation study, a two- to four-year break in employment lowers lifetime income by 13 percent; a five-year break lowers lifetime income by 19 percent.

Thus far, I've mostly been talking about corporate America, the sector that has the most visible and innovative work-family programs. On the low end of the work-family scale, there are no work-family programs. People in service or production jobs not only make less money than managers or professionals, but they almost always have much less flexibility. Consider the hypothetical case of a single mother who makes close to minimum wage as a chambermaid in a hotel. She's playing by the rules. She works hard. She isn't on welfare. But if her child is sick and she has to stay home from work, is her employer likely to cut her some slack? Not very.

In even worse shape are the growing number of "contingent" workers—freelance or temporary laborers who now make up 25 percent of the workforce. There are so many of them, frankly, because not having to give them health insurance, vacations, sick leave, or benefits of any kind makes them seem like a bargain. But it's fool's gold for corporate America. To really prosper, individual companies—and the country as a whole—will have to build a loyal, skilled, reasonably content workforce; and developing an unhealthy addiction to contingent workers is decidedly not the way to achieve this end.

It's all part of a larger shift in thinking the country is going to have to come to. As we approach the year 2000, I predict, more and more people will realize that the bottom-line worship of the past is counterproductive, a short-term fixation that will hurt us in the long run. They will see that employees aren't just workers, who disappear when the factory whistle blows, but people with full, rich, and complicated lives, and that when those lives are nurtured, everybody benefits.

The old saying used to go, What's good for General Motors is good for the country. How about changing it to, What's good for the *family* is good for the country?

CHAPTER IX

What *You* Can Do
for Your Family

The last three chapters have been about the family in relation to institutions: the government, corporations, schools, programs of every stripe. These will all be extremely important—indeed, vital—factors in determining the well-being of the American family as we approach the year 2000 and beyond. Nevertheless, ultimately, each family is on its own. Government agencies, social service programs, and benevolent employers all can help (just as their absence can hurt), but when all is said and done, the members of a family themselves determine whether it flourishes or withers or merely gets by. And, in turn, the collective strength and health of the millions of families in the country will determine the state of the American family as a whole.

In this final chapter, therefore, I want to stay close to the proverbial hearth and talk a little bit about how our own family ties can be bolstered. But it is only a chapter, so it will not contain a foolproof recipe for making your clan loving, harmonious, loyal, steadfast, and true. Entire books have been written on that subject, by authors more knowledgeable than I, and not one of us has gotten it right yet. And I've already made my feeling clear that, for the families in the most dire circumstances, the most significant thing needed is an improving economy that will provide better-paying jobs. What is more, neither I nor anyone else can provide a how-to manual for obtaining the two most vital qualities when it comes to nurturing a family: love and commitment. If you don't have them it's going to be a hard row to hoe. But if you do have the right foundation to build on, what you will find here are some suggestions about how to counter the late-twentieth-century trends that seem such powerful agents in fraying our family ties.

Earlier in the book, I've discussed many of the more profound of these trends: a tightening economy that causes both financial hardship and increased hours on the job for working parents; violence in the streets and on movie screens; high rates of divorce and out-of-wedlock birth. It seems to me that one set of statistics that sums up the problem is this: On average, fathers spend eight minutes a day talking—not nagging, yelling, or reminding, but talking—to their kids; working mothers spend eleven minutes; and even stay-at-home moms spend less than thirty minutes. Sad to say, the situation doesn't get much better on weekends, when the figure for dads only goes up to fourteen minutes.

So the first thing I would advise is to conduct a "conversation census" in your own family. Draw up a chart, and, for a whole week, have every adult carry a stopwatch and time how much talking they do with the kids. If you're not happy with the results, do something about it. Build some conversation time into the day, a time with no hurrying, chores, or schedules hanging over your head, when each of you can share what's on your mind. If it doesn't seem possible, don't just resign yourself to the situation. Seek guidance from the people affected—specifically, your children, spouse, and employer. And don't be surprised if one or all of them has some very helpful suggestions.

And, when it comes to the people closest to you, don't just ask for suggestions, ask for *them*. In times such as these "family" is going to have to be an elastic concept, one that can stretch to include close friends and relatives that go well beyond the insulated nuclear family of yore.

I think my own experience is instructive. I was a single parent for a while with Miriam, but even after Fred and I were married, we both worked. Since neither of us had much of an extended family, at least not in this country, we cultivated surrogate aunts and uncles and cousins and grandparents. Another way to look at it is that we revived the idea of unofficial godparents. The two friends who fit this role most were Dale and Al. They gave the kids the things we couldn't. Dale taught them about sports and the guitar. Al brought them to junkyards on Canal Street, buying bulbs and batteries and electronic equipment. Dale gave Joel a set of weights for his bar mitzvah, explaining that "He's not tall. He'll have to be well developed." I would never have thought of that. But it paid off, and now Joel is a magnificent skier.

It's not easy to find friends who are willing and able to fill such a role. Some people will say, "Oh, how are the kids?" and that's the last thing they want to hear about. But if you do have someone who you feel might be interested in occupying a special place in your child's life, don't be afraid to ask. And if the answer is yes, take advantage of a marvelous opportunity.

Of course the most obvious time that families spend together is at meals—specifically dinner. (Given the demands of everyone's schedule, a communal breakfast is too much to ask, and lunch is just about impossible.) In a recent national survey, 55 percent of the respondents said that gathering around the table for dinner was the most important way to bond family life. (Coming in second was family vacations, with 16 percent.) Another survey found that 82 percent of American families report eating together on a regular basis. That's fine, but in and of itself it's not enough. Consider: Only 45 percent reported that they turned off the television to make the meal more pleasant. The survey wasn't clear on whether 55 percent left the TV on, but whatever the case, a family dinner with television—or CDs, or radio, or telephone conversation, or newspaper reading—isn't really a family meal. I sometimes find it hard to understand why Americans seem to have such a need for background music, or background noise. Maybe it's to avoid silences. Comfortable silences, however, are simply a part of being together.

Sometimes, of course, silences are uncomfortable—as in the adolescent who seems determined not to let anyone "in." I've been there; I know this is not easy. My only suggestion is not to give up trying to draw teenagers out. Even though they act otherwise, they really do want to maintain a connection with you. So keep reaching out to them. The way to go is not open-ended questions; "How was your day?" is a real conversation stopper. It takes a little thought, but a better tack is something more specific, like "Do you like your Spanish teacher this year any better than the one you had last year?"

I'm not an Orthodox Jew, but when I think of the prototypical family meal, I always think of the Sabbath dinner. Everyone is hungry after synagogue, so it would be impossible for the food not to be satisfying. Turning on the radio or TV is not permitted, so there are no distractions. And cooking isn't allowed, either, so everything is prepared, leaving the family free to eat, converse, and be merry. Other religions have pleasant postworship meal rituals, too—just walk into almost any family restaurant in the United States on Sunday about noon, and you'll see what I mean.

I think people who don't participate in institutionalized religion can find a way to capture some of this feeling. The key element is ritual. So why not institute a family Sunday brunch, that can't be violated by soccer practice, business phone calls, or rock music?

Meals aren't only eaten—they have to be cooked first. Preparing food can be a wonderful family activity. Unfortunately, it's not taken advantage of very often. One of the surveys cited above revealed that 72 percent of the time, dinner is prepared by mother alone. If at all possible, get the family to pitch in and help. If it can't happen on weeknights, then be sure to set aside time on Saturday and/or Sunday. Kids love to eat food they've helped cook themselves, and if dad takes part, too, it's both a wonderful antidote to gender stereotyping and a model for a family working and cooperating together. The kitchen is also a place where multigenerational family traditions can be carried on and bolstered.

In implementing a family-togetherness strategy (to use a fancy term for something very simple), one of the first things that has to be confronted is television. As I discussed in an earlier chapter, ever since its earliest days, the TV has been portrayed alternately as a means of uniting families (the idea of the electronic hearth) and of pulling them apart (the image of Mom, Dad, Billy, and Sally each watching his or her own program on his or her own TV in his or her own room). As our kids were growing up, we only had one set, which led to some togetherness and a lot of fights over what should be on. Together, we learned to compromise.

There's no doubt about it: Americans, especially young Americans, watch too much television. Collectively, the country watches an estimated 120 billion hours of TV a year; preschool children watch an average of 30 hours a week. (As noted earlier, the average child spends a total of less than one hour a week conversing with his or her father.) All told, a child will spend 18,000 hours in front of the set by the time he or she graduates from high school, compared to 13,000 hours spent in the classroom. The really scary thing is that parents routinely underestimate the amount of TV their kids watch by 50 percent. Experts recommend that children be limited to ten hours of viewing a week, or at most two hours a day. Otherwise, not only will family bonding suffer, there will very likely be a detrimental effect on the child's attention span, language and communication skills, and creative abilities.

Recently, an organization called TV-Free America instituted an annual National TV-Turnoff Week, sponsored by such organizations as the American Federation of Teachers, the American Medical Association, and the Weekly Reader, in which people are urged to attempt seven days without TV cold turkey. I applaud this and similar efforts, especially in view of the fact that they tend to at least reduce the TV time of participants even when the week is over.

But people rarely keep the television off for good; it is by now a permanent fixture of our cultural landscape. No, the key is to harness the tremendous power of the medium, to make sure we control it as opposed to it controlling us. In terms of families, parents should certainly put a limit on the amount of TV their children watch, and monitor the contents. Beyond that, they should, whenever possible, watch TV together. One of the positive things about the medium is that it lends itself to being interactive. As opposed to being in a darkened movie theater, usually we watch television in a living room, and it seems perfectly natural to talk back to the set when some particularly idiotic commercial is on, or at least talk about it with the people watching with you. And that is a highly recommended activity for families. The best way to counter any negative influence of TV on kids is to get them to think, talk, and analyze.

Unfortunately, while traditionally there had been a great many shows appropriate for whole families to watch together—from *Bonanza* through *Bewitched* to *Cosby*—the trend is currently going in the other direction. For a few years, the networks made a laudable attempt to create an 8 to 9 P.M. "family hour," filling it with programs parents and children could watch together, but lately that has dissipated.

On the bright side, I put forth two words: *cable* and *video*. If you are fortunate enough to have cable service (and I recommend it as an investment for anyone with small children), you will find an abundance of high-quality educational material and wholesome entertainment on Nickelodeon, the Family Channel, the Learning Channel (TLC), the Discovery Channel, the Disney Channel, Arts & Entertainment (A&E), and elsewhere. And prerecorded videos, used wisely and in moderation (video watching is included in the two-hour-a-day limit recommended by experts), may be the perfect form of entertainment. Consider:

- As opposed to television, where anything is liable to come on (especially if the child has command of the channel-changer), the parent can completely control what is to be watched.
- There are plenty of tapes that are enjoyable for both parent and child, so it's very easy for viewing to be a shared activity. (Classic movie musicals like *The Sound of Music, The Wizard of Oz, The Music Man,* and *Annie* are especially good in this regard.)
- They can be turned off at any time, so viewing can be easily limited without the child missing anything.
- Most tapes can be rented, so you can "try before you buy."
- Best of all, there are no commercials.

So TV can be okay, and videos can be fine. But neither one is a substitute for reading. And especially when children are young, reading together and reading aloud is an absolutely essential family activity. For years, education experts have counseled that being read to—the most oftenly cited figure is twenty minutes a day—is the single most important factor in children's eventual success in reading on their own. Author Jim Trelease spread this gospel in *The Read-Aloud Handbook,* one of the best-selling books of the 1980s. One of Trelease's contributions is the idea of "listening level": a ten-year-old may be reading at a fourth-grade level but is able to comprehend much more advanced material that is read to her. It makes sense, and makes a perfect argument for the importance of reading aloud even to older kids.

Even though they came in second to meals in the aforementioned survey, vacations are a wonderful opportunity for family building. There's a Hebrew word, *chavayot,* that means a certain kind of emotional memories, and these are what the best vacations build. It's an experience you have that leaves an emotional residue; when you retrieve it, it has that warm glow.

In an article in the *New York Times,* writer Jan Benzel memorably and movingly described a quiet summer vacation where it seemed that nothing happened, but in reality was the setting for a multitude of momentous occurrences. I enjoyed the piece so much I'd like to share it with you.

I didn't make a pie again this summer. Or canoe across the salt pond on a steamy afternoon; or rent a Windsurfer for a morning's humiliation. The can of tennis balls is sitting un-opened on the hall table. The books are piled up, a couple half-read, by the low, wide bed with the pink and white quilt.

Each year, I try to cram real life—life that makes me feel most alive—into a few weeks away from work, away from the city. So much gets left out.

We didn't fly a kite; I didn't see a movie.

Here's what I did do: several hundred loads of laundry. Sheets and towels for friends and family. Folded little socks and T-shirts warm from the dryer, ready for another adventure in the backyard, another smear of ice cream. Chipped dried Play-Doh out of the holes of the cane-seat chairs. Found a suitable home for a delicate green grasshopper fond of climbing my daughter's silken hair. Ran in a rainstorm. Marveled at a turtle that wandered onto a friend's lawn. Scooped up sleepy-eyed children in the early Monday sunlight to see their father off at the train. Sang happy 70th birthday to my mother-in-law. Applied Band-Aids in neon colors. Stayed up late talking to a cherished friend, luxuriously uninterrupted by any of our collective four children who had finally fallen into bed. Shucked ears and ears of corn. Played Candyland.

The table in this rented house near the water is round, the envy of those with rectangular tables with their inherent hierarchy, round so that the conversation rolls from one person to the next as the food passes from hand to hand and disappears from the plates.

We feasted together on tomatoes, fish, bread, corn; reviving for the benefit of the youngest the age-old debate of the typewriter method of corn eating versus round-the-cob. The young ones, feeling grown up, practiced chewing with their mouths closed and other table manners, as if they were a new game.

I didn't write postcards or plant a garden or teach the girls to swim, or potty-train our 2-year-old or take away the pacifier she sleeps with. Time enough later to grow up.

We did have a picnic on the beach, trudging to a spot where we could see the ocean to the south and the sunset behind the pond. While others straggled off the beach, heading home salty-haired, we arrived, carting our beer and burgers, coolers and chips, ready for the chill of the evening in jeans and sweat shirts.

The girls made friends with children of picnickers down the beach, forming their own little society, swarming over an abandoned lifeguard stand they imagined into a clubhouse, leaving us to an ambivalent peace. We celebrated their independence, reveled in the unfamiliar ability to talk, and instantly missed the bony four-year-old elbows and knees of one and the baby belly and soft cheeks of her sweet small sister.

The children set free the turtle and the grasshopper, but it was mostly a summer for holding things close.

When I was their age, I climbed a towering stepladder to the low branches of my grandmother's sour-cherry tree and picked whatever the birds had missed. My mother made the cherries into pies. Nobody makes pies like my mother. Conditioned after raising six children, she still makes dessert from scratch almost every night, not knowing how many will show up with friends, still expecting dinner.

We bought a couple of pies from the fancy food places springing up. They're never quite right: the crust not flaky enough, the filling too sweet. "Pie's easy," my mother says. I don't think so.

The rolling pin goes back into the suitcase, along with the broken shells, the sandy shovels and pails. I'll lug it out next year, and probably not make a pie again.

We think of family vacations as involving young kids, but that doesn't have to be the case. Even now, with Joel and Miriam both adults with lives of their own, I try to arrange at least one trip a year where we all go away together. We are not alone, as I found out recently when I read an article in the *Philadelphia Inquirer* about adult children who continue to go on vacation with their parents. It featured the Glazer family of Wynnewood, Pennsylvania, who have an intriguing modus operandi when it comes to taking time off. Husband Bob's idea of a grand vacation is biking in the Canadian Rockies, while wife Susan's is to explore the streets of Taiwan. So while they sometimes travel together, they also go separately—taking along one or more of the three children.

I think it's a wonderful idea. Why drag a spouse along on a trip you love but that will make him or her miserable? When you get back, your spouse can enjoy the slides. Years ago, when the oldest was sixteen, Susan took the three kids to Greece and Israel. More recently, Bob took the youngest, Ted (who's now twenty-two), on a Colorado biking expedition. On one steep hill, Bob told the *Inquirer*, "I was holding him back. I told him to go on ahead, but he said, 'Heck, Dad, I want to be with you.' It makes me feel good. It's one of the rewards of being a parent."

Sensibly and laudably, the American tourism industry has recently made efforts to promote and facilitate family travel. Two hotel chains, Best Western and Hyatt, now have frequent-guest programs for children. Most resorts now have kid-friendly activity programs, and even Club Med, famous as an R-and-R spot for singles, now has six villages specifically designed for families. A still small but growing trend is grandparents taking their grandchildren on vacation. Club Med promotes to this group, as does the Grandtravel agency of Chevy Chase, Maryland, which offers an Alaska trip where you can ride dogsleds and learn how to build an igloo, and Kenya safari, and a rafting trip covering the Hoover Dam, the Grand Canyon, and the Colorado River.

Think all that stuff isn't appropriate for grandparents? You better smile when you say that, because you're talking to a grandmother who thinks it sounds fantastic!

The best vacations are like adventures, and my friend Pepper Schwartz, the sociologist who's a leading expert on couples and families, likes to talk about families who build such a sense of mutual adventure and teamwork into their day-to-day lives. "A lot of farm families have it," she told me. "I recently visited a horse farm in Kentucky and every element of the family that ran it was intensely involved in the enterprise—the grandfather, the sixty-year-old son, *his* sons and daughters. People who are cooperating in the same enterprise together always have more of a sense of being on the same team. It doesn't have to be a family business. It can mean being involved in your church, or a hobby like showing dogs. What you need is to share the same values, with the same intensity of purpose."

Pepper has incorporated these ideas into her own family life. She, her husband, and their two kids live on an island in Washington state. "We raise horses and llamas and sell them as pets and pack animals," she says. (That's in addition to her job as a professor, to which she has to commute by ferry, and her sociological research.) "It's very much a family thing. It gives the kids something to do that's serious. It really matters if the bunnies get fed. And it's fun, too—the kids take the baby llamas into town and show them off. This Friday, my daughter and I are going to a horse-trading seminar, and she's as intensely interested in it as I am. The whole enterprise gives them a sense of freedom and confidence and interaction with us that we find precious."

Some activities are specifically oriented toward the family. Reunions come immediately to mind. These annual get-togethers are a growing and wonderful trend in American society; in fact, Edith Wagner, the editor of *Reunions* magazine, estimates that about 200,000 of them are held every year. Of course, a "family reunion" can mean a group of eight or ten close relatives having coleslaw and ham sandwiches or it can mean a three-day, choreographed event, complete with fashion shows and seminars, at a large hotel with up to 2,000 participants.

The only two essentials, I would say, are plentiful food and drink and ample photo opportunities. If you're interested in putting a reunion together and are looking for other activities, I'd recommend picking up a copy of *The Family Reunion Handbook*, by Tom Ninkovich and Barbara E. Brown. Here are a few suggestions:

• Create and distribute T-shirts commemorating the reunion.
• Have an awards ceremony, with a prize given for every achievement you can think of: best pair of shoes, best report card (for the kids), closest family resemblance, and so on.
• Have adults bring in photographs of themselves as kids, and offer a prize for the family member who can identify the most photo subjects.
• Have some smart niece or nephew edit a video with clips from each individual family's personal collection (preferably with a few pratfalls included), for a presentation called "The ——— Family's Funniest Home Videos."

• Hold a storytelling session, with older relatives talking to the younger ones about events and people from the past. Make sure this is tape- or video-recorded for posterity.

Of course, this kind of oral-history making doesn't have to be limited to reunions; all you need are two people and a tape recorder. There's an African saying, "When an older person dies, it's as if a whole library is burned down." Taping oral histories is an excellent form of fire prevention. And not only will memories be preserved in the tapes, but the very act of conducting the interview will help build bridges of respect and affection across the generations. For tips on assembling an oral-history collection, see Bill Zimmerman's book *How to Tape Instant Oral Biographies*.

An activity that can be done in conjunction with the oral-history collection is assembling a family tree. It's easy to start: Just put the names of the youngest generation in the middle of the left-hand side of a big piece of paper, and start moving back in time. Of course, once you start going back a generation or two, there will be gaps and questions. To fill them in you'll have to consult the older generation—which itself is part of the point. Make sure that when you talk to them, you bring whatever photographs you possess; they're sure to jog even the foggiest memory. The more seriously you take it, and the more elaborate your family tree becomes, the more you'll have to start doing research in libraries, historical societies, and municipal archives for old birth certificates, marriage licenses, and citizenship papers. (If and when you come upon these documents, be sure to photocopy them so they can be preserved and shared with others.) Needless to say, this kind of detective work can be an exciting family adventure in and of itself.

One resource many have found invaluable is the Mormon Church's Family History Library in Salt Lake City, which houses the largest collection of genealogical material in the world—five centuries' worth of records on more than 2 billion people. The Church has gathered the information for theological reasons, but the records are open to anyone; indeed, most of the people who use them are non-Mormons. Nor do you necessarily have to travel to

Utah: Much of the information is available on computer in satellite libraries around the country.

Speaking of computers, there are numerous software programs available that will help you get your family tree as organized and spiffy looking as you could possibly want. Some of them are free or shareware and are available via ftp (file transfer protocol) at ftp.cac.psu.edu/pub/genealogy. One wonderful program that you'll have to pay about fifty dollars for is called Echo Lake. It's a kind of electronic family album, in which you can write down family memories, or even an elaborate family history, and illustrate them with art, photos, and even video and audio clips. The results can either be printed out or copied onto disks that can be viewed by other families, even if they don't have Echo Lake.

Moving back to genealogy for a minute, let me mention some other resources on the Internet. ROOTS-L is the largest electronic mailing list for people interested in finding their roots; to subscribe, send a message to listserv@vm1.nodak.edu with the single line subscribe roots-l Firstname Lastname. The largest Usenet newsgroup for genealogical information is soc.roots. And a World Wide Web site that can direct you to many other sources of information is the Genealogy Help and Guides page at http://ftp.cac.psu.edu/~saw/genealogy.html.

As the aforementioned should make abundantly clear, the information revolution has in many ways been a boon for families. What's really gotten the trend going in the past couple of years is children at college, who are provided with E-mail privileges free of charge. That in turn jump-starts the parents, and all of a sudden it's a cyberspace family. When family members are distributed around the country or the globe, as is so often the case nowadays, E-mail is a much cheaper way to stay in touch than phone calls and much easier than "snail mail." It's so irresistible, in fact, that it actually helps build family ties. The *Washington Post* recently ran an article about some fifty members of an extended family, living in such diverse locales as São Paulo, Brazil; Berkeley, California; and Corpus Christi, Texas, who had inaugurated their own computer network through Compuserve, and found that it led them to develop deeper relationships with many of their relatives than they ever had before. At the very least, it gives them a sense of belonging. One member of the network returned home from the hospital after giving birth and found forty-two messages waiting.

Computers aren't the only family-friendly technological innovation. Cellular phones may be fine for negotiating deals and impressing fellow diners in a restaurant, but they're a godsend when you're stuck in traffic and have to make sure that your child-care arrangements are taken care of. And while pagers may have the reputation of being a tool of the drug dealer's trade, they are essential in many of today's busy families. Some children are told to dial a parent's beeper number when they arrive after school, and punch in a prearranged code. For example, "1" may mean "I'm home," while "2" may mean, "I'm at Susie's house." Conversely, when the kid has a pager, the parent always has the capability of knowing where he or she is, or of transmitting the unspoken message, "It's time to come home now." In recognition of pagers' new role, they now come in purple, pink, and other funky colors.

MADE IN HEAVEN: MEET THE DINAPOLIS

Three brothers and two sisters, all married more than 50 years. Ben, Frank, and Joseph DiNapoli, Rita Scarcelle and Rose Canonaco. All told, 271 years of marriage. Consider that for a moment. Five siblings, all born more than 70 years ago, alive and happily married. Not only do the spouses still like one another, but the sisters-in-law and the brothers-in-law still like one another.

"We're old-timers. They don't make them like us anymore," says Ben DiNapoli, the oldest at 80 and the longest married at 57 years. "In our day, what you had, you kept. Divorce was a disgrace in the family."

Divorce is part of everyday life today, but not the DiNapolis' lives. Maybe it's religious conviction, because they are churchgoers after all. Too many of them to be luck. Maybe a statistical anomaly?

"The DiNapoli family is an easygoing and loving family," suggests Frank.

"The secret is talking about things, always talking," offers Clarence Scarcelle, Rita's husband of 55 years.

They grew up in Frankford and haven't strayed too far, all living in the Northeast, just minutes away from one another, in Somerton, Tacony, Bustleton, Burholme and Pennypack Park. Their parents, Louis and Clara, were married 52 years before he died, so perhaps there is a genetic disposition for long and happy marriages.

Louis—originally Luigi—came to Philadelphia in 1906 as a 17-year-old from Carosina, a little town near the heel of the boot in southern Italy.

In an Italian real-life version of *Cyrano de Bergerac,* Louis DiNapoli wrote love letters to a girl in Italy for an illiterate friend. "Then Mom sent a picture and my dad fell in love with the picture," says daughter Rita.

So he went back to Italy to see her and learned, to his delight, that she was in love with the man who wrote the letters. "But she was only 17 and her father told my father that he had older daughters."

But Louis had fallen in love with Clara, not her sisters. They married in Italy and he took his bride back to Philadelphia.

"In 1947, I went back to the church where they were married in 1911. I sat at the altar and talked to the same priest who married them," says Joseph, the youngest DiNapoli son, married just 52 years.

They all talk with great affection about Louis and Clara. "I remember my mother and father around the kitchen table, dancing," says Rita.

"My mother-in-law told me never to go to sleep if you've had an argument, unless you kiss and make up. You don't know. You may never wake up," says Diana DiNapoli, Joseph's wife. "I still dust off her picture every day. I still talk to her. My in-laws were beautiful people."

"My parents didn't have any money," says Frank. "Tuesday, Thursday and Sunday, we had spaghetti. Dad used to cut the hair of us kids and mend all the shoes. He was still cutting Ben's hair after Ben was married."

Ben—born Biagio—cannot get the words out as everyone laughs at the memory. He fires back at his little brother, who is 77: "And why not?"

Their father died in 1963, "two weeks before Kennedy," says Frank. Clara, who spent the last seven years of her life in a wheelchair, cared for by Rita and all the other DiNapolis, died four years later.

Frank DiNapoli met his wife, Gorizia—known as Goodie—when they were teenagers in Frankford.

"Clarence and I [that's Clarence Scarcelle, who would later marry Frank's sister, Rita] worked together in a leather shop. Clarence lived six blocks from me, and we used to sit in his car and the girls would come over and talk to us."

One of the girls was Gorizia. "I thought she was nice and I thought she was beautiful. Look at her."

He can still make her blush.

"I took her out Wednesdays, Saturdays and Sundays, but I was at her house every night. Took her out at 7 P.M., had her home by 10. We'd go to a 7 o'clock movie, go somewhere to pet and then home by 10."

He looks back on their wedding and says: "It was the thing in those days. Get married and have children."

They have two daughters and three granddaughters. "God blessed us with real good kids."

One of those kids—Clare—was home on a visit last month when she saw a notice of the wedding-anniversary Mass in church at St. Christopher's. "She told us to do it. I would have never thought of it."

"I'm excited about it," says Goodie.

"We lived through this 50 years and I didn't think we'd all make it. It's important to me," says Frank. "It's something to brag about."

A photographer poses the women on the men's laps, and there is the squealing laughter of newlyweds. An entreaty to kiss brings more delight. A question about sex after 50 years brings laughs and wisecracks. More stories are told about each other, about their folks, about the brother, Tom, who was married to Clarence Scarcelle's sister Martha. (They're both gone now—and they were married 45 years.) There are jokes about lost body shape and bad knees.

Most of all, there is love.

—Murray Dubin
The Philadelphia Inquirer

So far in this chapter—and in the book as a whole, really—I've concentrated on the "family" insofar as it involves children. Murray Dubin's wonderful story about the DiNapolis brings me to the other side of the coin: the importance for families of long-standing, loving relationships between two adults who are its head. I have no desire to denigrate single parents, and I certainly don't want to jump on the antidivorce bandwagon (I was divorced twice myself, after all), but I do believe that the backbone of the American family has always been and will continue to be strong, committed, long-term nuclear families. Even though I was divorced, my current marriage is going on forty years old, so I believe I am qualified to speak on the subject.

There has actually been surprisingly little research about the attributes of happy, successful, long-lasting relationships. (What's been done has, by necessity, focused on marriage, but it would apply to other long-term relationships as well.) One exception is the research of psychologist John Gottman, who has suggested that successful marriages occur when a balance is struck between positive and negative interactions. He posits a "magic number" of five positive exchanges for each negative one. Judith Wallerstein's recent book *The Good Marriage: How and Why Love Lasts,* argues that the key to a successful marriage is a couple's ability to grow and adapt to change. This in turn, she says, depends on mastering seven developmental tasks:

- Separating from the family of origin.
- Building intimacy while also simultaneously maintaining autonomy.
- Embracing the role of parents.
- Creating a safe haven to express conflict and even anger.
- Creating and maintaining a rich and satisfying sex life.
- Using humor.
- Never losing the romantic feelings of falling in love one had early in the relationship.

As for me, I would start my prescription with a rather unromantic statement: Nobody can fulfill *all* the needs of another person. Nor do I believe that when people get married, they should adopt the romantic notion that they should share *everything*. Mind you, I'm not saying that a husband or wife should go out and have an affair. It's never as easy as that.

But I am all in favor of maintaining separate interests. It's simply not true that the family that does everything together stays together. If people have their own work, their own interests, their own passions, so much the better for the relationship. On the other hand, if he loves opera and she detests it, it's a disaster if he drags her along to the Met.

The same goes for friends. I'm not always a believer in complete and total honesty, but in this case I am. If your husband's friend totally bores you, why should you torture yourself and be unhappy and miserable through fifty years of marriage? Admit it, and find ways of cultivating your friendships separately. Having said that, I'll also say you have to be careful. Let's say you go to the opera with a woman who's not your wife. The soprano begins to sing a beautiful aria and you feel very emotional. You put your arm around your companion and maybe there is some stirring of sensual feeling. On second thought, maybe it would be better to go with a whole *group* of people.

The common denominator is a relationship built on mutual liking, trust, respect, and loyalty. These thing do not just arrive on your doorstep, ready to unwrap; you have to nourish them constantly. One way to do so is by being inventive. That means not letting one day pass that's exactly like the day before. Each day you have to say, "I must do something to keep the relationship from going stale." You even have to work at finding new things to talk about. And you can *never* put the marriage or relationship on automatic pilot.

I like Wallerstein's emphasis on humor. As you get older, it becomes more and more necessary. If he starts getting a little paunch and starts losing his hair, and she has a waist that's not as it was before children, if they concentrate on that, the desire for any romantic inclinations flies out the window. No, you need a sense of humor to face life's vicissitudes, to keep that liveliness, that bouncing step, that heart that beats when the loved one walks in. The Talmud says that a lesson taught with humor is a lesson retained, and the sages knew what they were talking about.

Of course it's relatively easy to be loyal and committed through the good times; when hardship strikes, it's a challenge. And hardship will strike. That Ozzie-and-Harriet little white house in the suburbs, where nobody dies and nobody gets sick beyond a case of the sniffles—it's a lie. In every family, there will be storms to be weathered. With any luck, the family will emerge from the crisis or hard times more closely tied together than it was before. It's like that saying "Whatever doesn't kill me, makes me stronger." You can say, "Look, we survived this"—and that satisfaction will be productive for the family in the future.

What it all comes down to, I suppose, is the challenge of retaining—or restoring—the sense of lifelong commitment that was once the cornerstone of the family in a world that's changed in so many ways. Sadly, there's no magic formula. But happily, knowing that you want it is the most important single step toward achieving it. Humor is important, and so are a clear head, and shared values, and an ability to pace oneself. I'm talking about pacing yourself the way a long-distance runner does, and in a way a long relationship is like a cross-country race. There are uphill sections and downhill ones, bleak scenery and the most beautiful vistas. There are times when you feel so exhausted you want to stop running and quit the race. But if you pace yourself properly, and have the discipline to stay the course, you'll more than likely find that in the home stretch an exquisite "runner's high" kicks in, and it was all worth it.

For Further Reading

Anderson, Elijah. *Streetwise: Race, Class, and Change in an Urban Community.* Chicago: University of Chicago Press, 1990.

Bane, Mary Jo. *Here to Stay: American Families in the Twentieth Century.* New York: Basic Books, 1976.

Bellah, Robert N., Richard Madsen, William M. Sullivan, Ann Swidler, and Steven M. Tipton. *Habits of the Heart: Individualism and Commitment in American Life.* Berkeley: University of California Press, 1985.

Bennett, William J. *The De-Valuing of Family: The Fight for Our Culture and Our Children.* New York: Simon and Schuster, 1994.

Blankenhorn, David. *Fatherless America: Confronting Our Most Urgent Social Problem.* New York: Basic Books, 1995.

Burke, Phyllis. *Family Values: Two Moms and Their Son.* New York: Random House, 1993.

Cherlin, Andrew J. *Marriage, Divorce, Remarriage.* Cambridge: Harvard University Press, 1981.

Cherlin, Andrew J., ed. *The Changing American Family and Public Policy.* Washington, D.C.: Urban Institute Press, 1988.

Cherlin, Andrew J., and Frank Furstenberg. *The New American Grandparent: A Place in the Family, a Life Apart.* New York: Basic Books, 1986.

Clinton, Hillary R. *It Takes a Village: And Other Lessons Children Teach Us.* New York: Simon and Schuster, 1995.

Coontz, Stephanie. *The Social Origins of Private Life: A History of American Families 1600–1900.* London: Verso, 1988.

Coontz, Stephanie. *The Way We Never Were: American Families and the Nostalgia Trap.* New York: Basic Books, 1992.

Dizard, Jan E., and Howard Gadlin. *The Minimal Family.* Amherst: University of Massachusetts Press, 1990.

Furstenberg, Frank, and Andrew J. Cherlin. *Divided Families: What Happens to Children When Parents Part.* Cambridge: Harvard University Press, 1991.

Gutman, Herbert. *The Black Family in Slavery and Freedom.* New York: Oxford University Press, 1976.

Leach, Penelope. *Children First: What Our Society Must Do—and Is Not Doing—for Our Children Today.* New York: Alfred A. Knopf, 1994.

May, Elaine Tyler. *Homeward Bound: American Families in the Cold War Era.* New York: Basic Books, 1988.

Mintz, Steven, and Susan Kellogg. *Domestic Revolutions: A Social History of American Family Life.* New York: The Free Press, 1989.

Moynihan, Daniel P. *The Negro Family: The Case for National Action.* Washington, D.C.: U.S. Department of Labor, 1965.

Popenoe, David. *Disturbing the Nest: Family Change and Decline in Modern Societies.* New York: A de Gruyter, 1988.

Skolnick, Arlene. *Embattled Paradise: The American Family in an Age of Uncertainty.* New York: Basic Books, 1991.

Spigel, Lynn. *Make Room for TV: Television and the Family Ideal in Postwar America.* Chicago: University of Chicago Press, 1992.

Stacey, Judith. *Brave New Families: Stories of Domestic Upheaval in Late Twentieth Century America.* New York: Basic Books, 1991.

Taylor, Ella. *Prime-Time Families: Television Culture in Postwar America.* Berkeley: University of California Press, 1989.

Thurer, Shari. *The Myths of Motherhood: How Society Reinvents the Good Mother.* Boston: Houghton Mifflin, 1994.

Trelease, Jim. *The Read-Aloud Handbook.* New York: Penguin, 1982.

Wallerstein, Judith, and Sandra Blakeslee. *The Good Marriage: How and Why Love Lasts.* Boston: Houghton Mifflin, 1995.

Wallerstein, Judith, and Joan B. Kelly. *Surviving the Breakup: How Children and Parents Cope with Divorce.* New York: Basic Books, 1990.

Weissbourd, Bernice, and Sharon Lynn Kagan, eds. *Putting Families First: America's Family Support Movement and the Challenge of Change.* San Francisco: Jossey-Bass, 1994.

Westheimer, Ruth, and Steven Kaplan. *Surviving Salvation: The Ethiopian Jewish Family in Transition.* New York: New York University Press, 1992.

Wilson, William Julius. *The Truly Disadvantaged: The Inner City, the Underclass, and Public Policy.* Chicago: University of Chicago Press, 1987.